Sailing Through the Storms of Life

- Practical Steps To Overcoming Your Crisis -

Sailing Through the Storms of Life

- Practical Steps To Overcoming Your Crisis -

by
Ronald H. Clark, D. Min.

Living Water Publishing Company
Tampa, Florida

Unless otherwise indicated, all Scripture quotations are taken from the *New King James Version* of the Bible. Copyright © 1979, 1980, 1982, Thomas Nelson, Inc., Publishers.

Scriptures marked AMP are taken from *The Amplified Bible, Old Testament*, copyright © 1965, 1987 by The Zondervan Corporation, Grand Rapids, Michigan, or *The Amplified Bible, New Testament*, copyright © 1958, 1987 by The Lockman Foundation, La Habra, California.

Scriptures marked KJV are taken from *The King James Version* of the Bible.

Sailing Through the Storms of Life
Practical Steps To Overcoming Your Crisis
ISBN 0-9641920-0-4
Copyright © 1994 by
Ronald H. Clark Ministries
Library of Congress Catalog Card Number: 94-77928

Published by
LIVING WATER PUBLISHING COMPANY
6850 Living Water Place
Tampa, FL 33610

Printed in the United States of America. All rights reserved under International Copyright Law. Contents and/or cover may not be reproduced in whole or in part in any form without the express written consent of the Publisher.

Dedication

To my lovely wife, Belinda, my sailing partner with whom many of these life-changing principles were discovered, and also to my son, Wilson, and daughter, Amanda, who have brought so much joy to us as we sail through life.

Acknowledgements

I want to recognize the wonderful church staff the Lord Jesus has given Living Water Church, especially those particular helpers who assisted with the book: Rev. Jane Hillman, Associate Pastor/Administrator, for assisting in the editing; Associate Pastors Leon van Rooyen and Roger Fields for assisting in polishing the final manuscript; my secretary Jenny McCord for coordinating production, and Tracey Meister for typing. The support of our many friends and from Living Water Church has been such a blessing. Thank you, Belinda and I love you all!

Contents

Foreword		9
Introduction		11
1	Perilous Times Are Here!	13
2	Strengthening Your Confidence in God's Word	19
3	Closing The Door to Fear and Panic	31
4	Staying Strong in Crisis	35
5	How Jesus Handled Crisis — Managing a Crisis	41
6	Crisis Checklist	49
7	Assuming Personal Responsibility	53
8	Breaking Bad Habits That Create Crisis!	65
9	Cleaning Up Stinking Thinking!	85
Afterword		95

Foreword

I would like to highly recommend Dr. Ron Clark's book, *Sailing Through the Storms of Life*.

In this book, Ron gives some practical examples of what to do when the storms of life come. We know the storms of life come to everyone, and it is important what you do when the winds and the waves are contrary and the situation looks bleak. Scripture teaches us in Psalm 34:19, **Many are the afflictions of the righteous, but the Lord delivers him out of them all.**

I know that this book will be a great blessing to you as it has been to me in reading this manuscript. Ron is not only a respected Pastor of a powerful church, but also my close and dear friend.

>   Dr. Rodney M. Howard-Browne
>   President, R.H.B.E.A., Inc.
>   Louisville, Kentucky

Introduction

The pulse of this very hour is that tremendous things are happening in the earth. Wonderful things! Supernatural things! This is the most exciting time to be alive in the history of the world. You were born for **such a time as this** (Esther 4:14).

Running parallel to the great things that are happening are the great stress and changes that are taking place. But you can be assured, the Holy Spirit Who is in your life, is equal to the task at hand. If God did not think you could survive the age in which we are living, He would never have put you in this hour.

Because of the seriousness of the hour, I want to share with you how to stand through a time of crisis, so you are personally prepared to overcome, and so you also can help others overcome their crises.

James 4:8 says, **Cleanse your hands, you sinners; and purify your hearts, you double-minded.** First Peter 1:16 says, **Be holy, for I am holy.** Besides knowing how to manage a crisis, preparation for this hour involves growing up spiritually in correcting attitudes, in assuming responsibilities, in shaking off bad habits and in replacing stinking thinking with meditation of God's Word.

Above all, I pray this book will infuse you with a spirit of hope and joy that, regardless of the circumstances you may be facing, you can live above the circumstances and always triumph when you walk hand in hand with Jesus Christ, your Lord and Savior. **Now thanks be to God who *always* leads us in triumph in Christ, and through us diffuses the fragrance of His knowledge in every place** (2 Cor. 2:14).

Dr. Ronald H. Clark

1
Perilous Times Are Here!

> But know this, that in the last days perilous times will come.
>
> 2 Timothy 3:1

Prophetically, Paul is giving a description of the hour we are in right now. In the natural, great stress has come upon the earth.

Verses 2-7 indicate what the result of perilous times will be:

> For men will be lovers of themselves, lovers of money, boasters, proud, blasphemers, disobedient to parents, unthankful, unholy,
>
> Unloving, unforgiving, slanderers, without self-control, brutal, despisers of good,
>
> Traitors, headstrong, haughty, lovers of pleasure rather than lovers of God,
>
> Having a form of godliness but denying its power. [In other words, they may attend church and riot all in the same weekend!] **And from such people turn away!**
>
> For of this sort are those who creep into households and make captives of gullible women loaded down with sins, led away by various lusts,
>
> Always learning and never able to come to the knowledge of the truth.

We must learn to manage the times of stress that have come and those that will yet come upon the earth. To *manage* means "to direct, control, or handle; to make submissive." If we do not learn how to manage crisis, it will manage us. If we do not learn how to control the circumstances that are going on around us, the circumstances will control us. It's time for us to learn how to make the circumstances be submissive to us. It is not the will of God for circumstances to be out of control. You can make every crisis submissive to the Word of God.

Crisis means "a time of intense stress, a turning point." The turning point can be good or it can be bad, but it depends upon your management of the crisis. As a born-again believer, you have control over the crises!

I have seen good people allow a time of stress to tear their family or their church up, blowing the marriage or church family to pieces. The destruction of your family, the church, the community and the institutions that are around you is not the will of God. On the other hand, I have seen people grow stronger in faith during a time of great stress.

God is not a respecter of persons. We all tend to think we are the only one who goes through certain problems, but the Scripture teaches us "[All] temptation is common to man...." (1 Cor. 10:13.) Notice, *He* makes a way out of crisis times for all of us who believe and trust Him. He wants you and me to know how to control a crisis.

The word *perilous* means "hard to deal with, difficult, painful and grievous." In the last days, which is the very hour in which we are living, times will get difficult and hard to deal with, but not impossible to deal with as we yield to the direction and anointing of the Holy Spirit.

God's promises do not change just because a crisis shows up! **For I am the Lord, I do not change** (Mal. 3:6). His Word remains the same. Proverbs 3:26 says, **For the Lord will be your confidence, and will keep your foot from being caught.** Proverbs 14:26 says, **In the fear** [or worship] **of the Lord there is strong confidence, and His children will have a place of refuge.** Hebrews 10:35,36 says,

Therefore do not cast away your confiden
great reward. For you have need of endura
after you have done the will of God, you may re
promise.

Crisis comes when you stop believing God's promises. It comes when the Lord is not your confidence, and you think your foot will be caught. Circumstances turn into crises when you do not feel there is any place of refuge for you to run to in a time of trouble. Crisis comes when you cast away your confidence, which has great reward. If you cast away your confidence, you will lose the reward of it. The reward is the fulfillment of the promises in God's Word that you have been standing on. If you throw away your confidence in God, His promises will not work for you.

Crisis becomes destructive as a result of an erosion of our confidence in what God says. In other words, you are overcome by a crisis if you stop believing God will fulfill His promises in your life. You will be overcome in a time of crisis if you think you are going to fail. Regardless of how bad the circumstances are, they will not become a crisis until you think you are going to fail. When you begin to entertain thoughts of failure, you will be overcome by the crisis.

In Luke 6:47-49, Jesus compares the person who builds on the Rock of the Word to the person who is a doer of the Word:

Whoever comes to Me, and hears My sayings and does them, I will show you whom he is like:

He is like a man building a house, who dug deep and laid the foundation on the rock. And when the flood arose, the stream beat vehemently against that house, and could not shake it, for it was founded on the rock.

But he who heard and did nothing is like a man who built a house on the earth without a foundation,

against which the stream beat vehemently; and immediately it fell. And the ruin of that house was great.

A storm in life will test the validity and reality of your faith. Notice storms come to both those who are ready and those who are not. Sitting in church does not test your faith. All believers look the same without pressure. They attend church, raising their hands in worship, but the similarities end when the *pressure* is on!

If Christians collapse quickly when faced with a stormy circumstance, their foundation or confidence in God's Word is eroding. We need to stand in the face of any circumstance. If the whole world's economy collapses, we are determined to believe God can take care of us. We will not be moved. If our community erupts in a war, we are going to stand. If ten thousand fall at our right hand, we are standing. We will not be moved. We will not draw back. We will not compromise. We are standing on the Rock. What is the Rock? Some say Jesus. It is Jesus, but it is more. The Rock is *obedience to His Word*. To doubt His Word and not obey, is to doubt *Him* and not obey Him. He said in John 14:21, **He who has My commandments and keeps them, it is he who loves Me.**

Job said, **Though He slay me, yet will I trust Him** (Job 13:15). Job didn't have the revelation of the character of God that you and I have, but his attitude of obedience, regardless of circumstances, is one we all should maintain. God doesn't murder anyone. John quotes Jesus, **The thief** [Satan] **does not come except to steal, and to kill, and to destroy. I** [Jesus] **have come that they may have life, and that they may have it more abundantly** (John 10:10). When you see stealing, killing, and destruction, you know who's been there: the thief, the killer, the destroyer.

Regardless of the circumstances you are facing and the spiritual forces behind them, it is your choice to continue to trust and serve the Lord. The Word teaches us in Psalm 34:17, **The Lord hears, and delivers them out of all their troubles.**

Maintain your confidence in crisis by getting a proper perception of the problem. Bring the problem into context with what God says, realizing that He will not allow the problem to last forever. See yourself making it. See yourself coming through into victory.

Accurate Perception of the Problem

Strong faith in God's Word will cause you to get an *accurate perception of the problem*. When you look at the problem through the Word, you see the problem the way God does, through His eyes. Remember, 1 Corinthians 10:13 says, **No temptation has overtaken you except such as is common to man; but God is faithful, who will not allow you to be tempted beyond what you are able, but with the temptation will also make the way of escape, that you may be able to bear it.**

You can bear any temptation or trial when you know God is going to make a way of escape for you. You can go through anything if you know it is going to turn out all right. Romans 8:28 says, **And we know that all things work** (a process) **together for good to those who love God, to those who are the called according to His purpose.** In other words, do what He says. If you lose your confidence in God in the middle of a temptation or a trial, you will collapse.

Though some preachers may teach you how to *endure*, I want you to learn how to *escape* and *overcome*, not just hang in there. There is no virtue in just enduring pressure. The joy comes when you get out of it. Remember, crisis will never leave you the same. It's a turning point!

2
Strengthening Your Confidence in God's Word

James 1:3 says, **Knowing that the testing of your faith produces patience.** The *testing* of your faith literally means to test the trustworthiness of your faith. It means that when you are facing a trial, what is being tested is, *how trustworthy is that which you believe*? Most people get exactly what they are believing for!! If we believe we'll fail, it is amazing how often we will fall short of God's highest and best for our life. What is even sadder is many are taught that failure is the will of God! Some believe heaven is the only place we reap. But, for example, what need is there of money or health in heaven? The streets are paved with gold and you'll have a glorified body. What good is victory over the devil when he is cast into the bottomless pit and all his cronies with him? We need to experience victory *now* on earth!

It doesn't take anything to say, "God is a Healer, or God can heal!" But it takes a lot of confidence to believe that He is your Healer when you are facing sickness and disease.

James 1:12 says, **Blessed is the man who endures temptation; for when he has been approved** [or when he has made it through], **he will receive the crown of life which the Lord has promised to those who love Him.** First Peter 4:12 says, **Beloved, do not think it strange concerning the fiery trial which is to try you, as though some strange thing happened to you.** In other words, you can expect the enemy to try to steal your confidence in God. Remember, confidence in God is confidence in His Word which is the revelation of His will. He reveals how we will get through these circumstances with His help.

An example of this is found in Numbers 13. Moses was getting ready to lead the people of Israel into the promised land. He sent out twelve spies. They brought back a report that the land was all that God had promised and that it flowed with milk and honey. The problem was the land was inhabited by an enemy they would have to dispossess! Ten came back and said, "We can't make it. We are like grasshoppers in the sight of these giants. It's impossible."

Because of this bad report, the people lost heart, and they began to faint and grumble. "Moses, did you bring us out here to die?" First of all, Moses didn't bring them anywhere. God did. A pillar of fire (symbol of the anointing of the Holy Spirit) led them. Does God ever lead anyone into defeat? My Bible says, **Now thanks be to God who always leads us in triumph in Christ** (2 Cor. 2:14). A bad report robbed the Israelites of their confidence in what God had promised them and now they were facing a crisis.

The other two spies, Joshua and Caleb, after seeing the identical circumstances the ten spies had seen, came back and said, **Let us go up at once and take possession, for we are well able to overcome it** (Num. 13:30). They believed what God said, despite their circumstances.

The majority prevailed and the majority failed. Joshua and Caleb were the only two of the twelve spies who remained alive and entered into the promised land. The ten bearing the evil report died by a plague. (Num. 14:37.) (God takes no pleasure if we shrink back.)

There are believers today who are in a wilderness experience because something happened that robbed them of their confidence in God. Now they are wandering around, unable to move into the *best* that God has for them.

In 2 Kings 6, Elisha was surrounded by a great army. His servant went out to get a bucket of water to cook breakfast. He walked outside the hut and there were enemy troops surrounding him. This is called stress! That's a lot of enemy troops to wake up to! The servant came back in a panic! You know that's not the Holy Spirit. That was the servant's flesh talking! He began to believe what he could see was stronger than God! (Remember what you see is subject to change.) He was overwhelmed by the enormity of the problem.

> And when the servant of the man of God arose early and went out, there was an army, surrounding the city with horses and chariots. And his servant said to him, "Alas, my master! What shall we do?"
>
> So he [Elisha] answered, "Do not fear, for those who are with us are more than those who are with them."
>
> And Elisha prayed, and said, "Lord, I pray, open his eyes that he may see." Then the Lord opened the eyes of the young man, and he saw. And behold, the mountain was full of horses and chariots of fire all around Elisha.
>
> 2 Kings 6:15-17

If you will keep an accurate perception of everything you are facing, realizing God is bigger than any problem, you will never allow a crisis to overtake you! God does not respond to need (if He did, the starving children of Cambodia would be the most spiritual and blessed). He responds to our faith! Our *trust* and obedience in what He has said in His Word!

Maintaining a Support Network

To have a strong foundation, you must maintain a strong network of support. Galatians 6:2 says, **Bear one another's burdens, and so fulfill the law of Christ.** Hebrews 10:25 says, **Not forsaking the assembling of ourselves together, as is the manner of some, but** exhorting one another, and so much the more as you see the Day approaching. When you get under pressure or you are in a crisis, it is the worst time for you to stop going to church. (It's important to go to a church that teaches the Word and its application for victory.)

When people get under pressure, you will find out real quick what is in their foundation. If their foundation isn't strong when Satan attacks, usually the first thing they do is stop going to church and start blaming God for the trouble. When you are under pressure and all hell has seemingly broken loose against you, you ought to increase the number of times you go to church rather than decrease it. You need the support of Bible-believing friends!

When finances dry up and there is trouble in your marriage and family, it's time to run *to* the church, not *from* it. Make a decision, "I am going whether I feel like it or not." Don't allow the enemy to think that trouble can drive you away from your church when circumstances are getting worse. Your commitment to God and His goodness needs to remain strong regardless of circumstances.

God says of you, **I** [you] **shall not die, but live, and declare the works of the Lord** (Ps. 118:17). That's what God says, but you won't get that from the TV or out of the newspaper. These are not going to encourage your faith in God's Word! You will get that in church. Your faith will grow **by hearing, and hearing by the** *Word of God* (Rom. 10:17).

If you are not hearing the Word, your faith isn't being built up and if your faith isn't being strengthened, the enemy will attempt to erode your confidence in God's Word. Trials and tests will cause you to collapse if you allow your confidence to weaken.

Patience in the Face of Opposition

Another important factor is to remain patient in the time of opposition. Luke 21:19 says, **By your patience**

possess your souls. The only way to get control of your soul — your mind, will and emotions — is with patience. Patience is the result of faith. It is a spiritual force that proceeds out of your spirit (Gal. 5:22). It is God's powerful response to fear and worry.

Hebrews 11:1 says, **Now faith is the substance of things hoped for, the evidence of things not seen.** In other words, faith believes God's Word until it receives what was promised. Faith holds on until the promise manifests. Faith holds on until circumstances line up with what God has promised. Faith believes the Word despite contrary circumstances. When you know God is helping you overcome, you will have the ability to endure anything.

Hebrews 10:36 says, **For you have need of endurance, so that after you have done the will of God, you may receive the promise.** The *Amplified Translation* of this verse says, **For you have need of steadfast patience and endurance, so that you may perform and fully accomplish the will of God, and thus receive and carry away [and enjoy to the full] what is promised.**

You and I must hang in there! We can't quit! What do you have to go back to? The children of Israel wanted to go back to Egypt (to them, old life) and trust that the enemy would be merciful, rather than believe in God's ability to get them through. The only place you can go is to God and *hold on to Him.*

> **Therefore we also, since we are surrounded by so great a cloud of witnesses, let us lay aside every weight, and the sin which so easily ensnares us, and let us run with endurance the race that is set before us.**
> **Hebrews 12:1**

Stay Confident in God's Integrity

God has put His Word above His Name! In other words, His Word is as good as His name! Keep confessing your confidence in God's Word. First Peter 5:7 says, **Casting all your care upon Him, for He cares for you.** How do you cast your care on the Lord? You cast your cares with what you say. Hebrews 4:14 says, **Seeing then that we have a great High Priest who has passed through the heavens, Jesus the Son of God, let us hold fast our confession.**

Confession means "to say the same thing God says." What does God say about the challenge you are facing? Find out what the Bible says about the challenge and confess God's promises. Don't walk by how you feel. *Walk by what God says.*

Does God ever say, "You are not going to make it?" No! That's why you need to say what God says. Find promises related to your problem and believe them. Act on them. Speak them. Get a mental picture of what it will look like when God is done! Your foundation must be based on confessing what God says.

Imagine that you are at the last game of the world series, the seventh game, and it is tied. It's the bottom of the ninth inning, the bases are loaded, the pitcher pitches the ball, the catcher catches the ball and the umpire says nothing. Thirty seconds go by and the crowd is hushed. A minute goes by and the people begin to murmur. Five minutes go by and they're saying, "What is it?" The umpire raises his hand and says, "It's nothing until I call it." In other words, the game is not over until the umpire speaks. Technically, the game will not end until the umpire makes a decision to end it.

Similarly, your game is not over until you say it's over. When you say, "I can't go on," you can't go on. If you say, "I am not going to make it," you're not going to make it. If you say, "It will never happen," you have called your own game. If you can't call it like God calls it, the best thing for you to do is not to say anything. Make the enemy wait and wonder. Make him fret and worry, but don't say anything until you can say what God says.

The peace of God is your umpire. The Scripture says to let the peace of God rule in your heart. The Greek word *rule* means act as an umpire. When you lose your peace, don't make a decision. If you do, it will probably be wrong.

Mark 4:19 says, **And the cares of this world, the deceitfulness of riches, and the desires for other things entering in choke the word, and it becomes unfruitful.** Cares and distractions, which both mean to be drawn in a different direction, will choke out the Word. It will choke out your confidence in God's Word.

When you are moving in a positive faith direction, cares and distractions, if allowed, will entangle you and cause you to turn and go in the wrong direction. They will cause your priorities to change. You can be moved off course by the deceitfulness of riches and the desire for other things. The way to lose your direction is to think more of the "things" than you do of God Who gave you the things; to put money ahead of the God Who provides for you, or to desire certain things more than you desire to worship the Lord; these things will erode your confidence in God.

Care will move you in the wrong direction. Cares can captivate your imagination. Pretty soon, you are thinking more about the care than God. Care also comes in the form of activities. These activities can steal your time to worship the Lord, which will eventually cause an erosion in the foundation of your confidence in God. Many activities are okay in their place, but when they are out of priority, they will eventually choke out higher priorities.

We should go to church, not because of need, but because we want to give of ourselves. We want to worship and serve the Creator and keep ourselves in the love of God. If you let that support begin to erode, the first thing you will do is start increasing the hours at work and it starts choking out the time you used to spend reading your Bible, praying, going to church, or serving the Lord Jesus. Distractions will steal the important time that you used to call your neighbors and encourage them, or take your wife on a date, it robs you of the time you used to share the goodness of God with other people. All of these cares will begin to choke out the things of God in your life.

Start casting your cares upon the Lord. Care more about what He cares about! This will help you keep a proper perspective and remain patient under pressure.

Have you ever run short of money? Did worry add one dollar to it? It is better to give God that care and keep serving Him. If we don't look at our problems with God's view, we will worry about everything. "Oh, my God, what are we going to do?" Worry magnifies the problem in the same way that worship magnifies God.

Another way the enemy steals your confidence in the Word is found in Matthew 13:21, which says, **Yet he has no root in himself, but endures only for a while. For when tribulation or persecution arises because of the word, immediately he stumbles.** When you start growing in faith, Satan will attack you to get the Word out of you. He wants to rob it, steal it, or like a bird, just snatch it right out of your life. Pretty soon the tribulation and persecution become like giants — bigger than God.

What is the first thing Satan does to try to rob you of your confidence in God? It starts with a difficulty. In other words, dangers or difficulties erode your confidence in God. Something goes wrong. It's not in the plan. It's not good (it doesn't even have to be big).

Have you ever seen the work of termites? They leave the paint on the outside, but inside there is nothing there. They eat away on the inside, and they destroy the foundation. The same thing occurs on the inside of you when you let the situation take your confidence, your faith, and allow fear to take its place. Faith says God is taking care of me today. Fear says He's not.

Having God's perspective is how you endure pressure. What happens when you face difficulties or some problem pokes a hole in you, revealing some of your weaknesses? I've seen people who appear to have everything together on the outside, but you drop a dish or spill a glass of milk in their home and they explode. It's not the glass of milk or the dish that did it. That's just a little hole revealing that something is wrong on the inside. When you start exploding at little things, go back and check your heart, what's bugging you? I have found that when people are under great pressure, and they're not giving it to God, they react to little things that normally wouldn't affect them. Remember, *casting* all of your cares means God has all the cares and you keep none for yourself.

I received a letter that said, "Pastor, you don't love me." I contacted the person and said, "I think there is more to this. I have never done anything to indicate to you that I don't love you." "Yeah, but you didn't speak to me the other day." The truth is, "I didn't see you!" I wanted to find out what was really going on. *Why* were they acting so insecure? When I dug below the paint level, I found out I wasn't the real issue. There was something going on. The person needed to know everything was going to work out, but they reacted to a little thing that didn't even exist. When we got to the root of the problem and applied God's Word, the insecurity left.

When you become over-sensitive, start looking at what you think most about. That's the time to go back to church, recommit yourself, go Sunday morning, Sunday night and Wednesday night, go to prayer on another day and begin to fill your thoughts with the truth and not the lies of the enemy or even your own imagination. I usually say, "I'm not going to let this thing dictate to me. I am going to manage it. That means it is going to do what I say and I say what God says! *He is always right*! I am going to start confessing my confidence in God."

You may not feel like it and the devil may say, "I don't think it's going to work out all right," but God knows it will work out if you hang in there, obey Him and just say what He says!

Hebrews 3:6 says, **But Christ as a Son over His own house, whose house we are if we hold fast the confidence and the rejoicing of the hope firm to the end.** Hope believes that everything is going to turn out all right. Hope says, "God can do it." Faith says, "God will do it for me now."

Begin to thank God that everything is going to be all right, even though it may not look like it. Hold on to your hope, firm unto the end. The end is when you get what you are hoping for.

Hebrews 3:14 says, **For we have become partakers of Christ if we hold the beginning of our confidence steadfast to the end.** This means you can hold on to the confidence you had in God before the crisis hit, until the day the problem is resolved. Don't ever lose your hope, because God will never fail you.

Isaiah 41:10-13 (AMP) says:

Fear not; [there is nothing to fear] (if God is on your side), **for I am with you; do not look around you in terror and be dismayed, for I am your God. I will strengthen and harden you to difficulties, yes, I will help you; yes, I will hold you up and retain you with My [victorious] right hand of rightness and justice.**

Behold, all they who are enraged and inflamed against you shall be put to shame and confounded; they who strive against you shall be as nothing and shall perish.

> You shall seek those who contend with you but shall not find them; they who war against you shall be as nothing, as nothing at all.
>
> For I the Lord your God hold your right hand; I am the Lord, Who says to you, Fear not; I will help you!

Numbers 23:19 makes a strong statement, revealing God's unchanging integrity.

> God is not a man, that He should lie, nor a son of man, that He should repent. Has He said, and will He not do? Or has He spoken, and will He not make it good?

Hebrews 10:35 says, **Therefore do not cast away your confidence, which has great reward.** The reward of your confidence is that everything is going to be all right! With *promises* like these, how can we lose!

A lack of *confidence* makes you vulnerable for Satan to take advantage of you. When your faith breaks down, it leaves you open to attack. Once you have lowered your shield of faith, Paul tells us in Ephesians 6:10-13, the fiery darts of the wicked one will begin to penetrate. You will begin to consider the possibility that you might not make it, which will erode your foundation and shake your stand of full confidence in God. God's promises are forever settled in heaven (Ps. 119:89), which means they will never change. You are the one who changes. Circumstances can change, but God never changes.

3
Closing the Door to Fear and Panic

Second Corinthians 4:8,9 says:

We are hard pressed on every side, yet not crushed; we are perplexed, but not in despair;
Persecuted, but not forsaken; struck down, but not destroyed.

When you begin to consider that you might be destroyed, then you are very vulnerable to attack and the flood gates of hell will open up against you. Job said, **For the thing I greatly feared has come upon me, and what I dreaded has happened to me** (Job 3:25). There is no room for fear for the person standing in faith, believing and speaking God's promises, for fear and faith are opponents. Fear believes the worst will happen, faith believes the best. The Scripture says, **For God has *not* given us a spirit of fear, but of power and of love and of a sound mind** (2 Tim. 1:7).

When you are in fear, you are depleted and weak mentally, physically, but especially spiritually and things are falling apart all around you, and as a result this crisis situation, being out of proportion, becomes destructive, and now panic sets in!

In Matthew 14, Peter hit a crisis. Let's look at this account in verses 22-33:

Immediately Jesus made His disciples get into the boat and go before Him to the other side, while He sent the multitudes away.
And when He had sent the multitudes away, He went up on a mountain by Himself to pray. Now when evening came, He was alone there.

But the boat was now in the middle of the sea, tossed by the waves, for the wind was contrary.

Now in the fourth watch of the night Jesus went to them, walking on the sea.

And when the disciples saw Him walking on the sea, they were troubled, saying, "It is a ghost!" And they cried out for fear.

But immediately Jesus spoke to them, saying, "Be of good cheer! It is I; do not be afraid."

And Peter answered Him and said, "Lord, if it is You, command me to come to You on the water."

So He said, "Come." And when Peter had come down out of the boat, he walked on the water to go to Jesus.

Now, here is Peter's crisis....

But when he saw that the wind was boisterous, he was afraid; and beginning to sink he cried out, saying, "Lord, save me!"

Now, here is Jesus' response to Peter's crisis....

And immediately Jesus stretched out His hand *and caught him*, and said to him, "O you of little faith, why did you doubt?"

And when they got into the boat, the wind ceased.

Then those who were in the boat came and worshiped Him, saying, "Truly You are the Son of God."

If you are in a crisis right now, you can cry out to the Lord, "Save me." When you cry out to the Lord, those who are in the boat watching you may criticize you, but don't listen to them. Keep your eyes on Jesus, He will rescue you. (Remember, the disciples made no attempt to help Peter, only Jesus did.) First Peter 3:12 says **For the eyes of the Lord are on the righteous, and His ears are open to their prayers.** Our perspective should be, "We have a big God and little problems."

The Flesh Incites Panic!

Your flesh only believes what it hears, feels, sees, smells, tastes, and senses. Your spirit man believes what God says, no matter what the senses say. If you listen to your senses, panic sets in and that means your flesh is in control.

Romans 8:8,9 says:

> **So then, those who are in the flesh cannot please God.**
>
> **But you are not in the flesh but in the Spirit, if indeed the Spirit of God dwells in you. Now if anyone does not have the Spirit of Christ, he is not His.**

In other words, let the Holy Spirit control your life through the Word of God. The Word will reprogram fleshly, fearful thoughts. Second Corinthians 10:4 says, **For the weapons of our warfare are not carnal but mighty in God for pulling down strongholds.** The strongholds are in your mind. You pull them down by believing what God says when your thinking does not agree. When your flesh speaks, based on the senses, "I am not going to make it," your spirit says, "The Word says I am going to make it." If you are Spirit-led, you will not allow your fleshly thoughts to control you. You will let the Spirit control you with what God says.

When you get into the flesh and let the crisis circumstances take hold of you, you will become agitated and fall back on old coping habits (coping is learning to put up with negative circumstances) — the ones you had in your life prior to your commitment to Christ. That means if you used to drink, if the pressure is great enough, you will go back to drinking to cope with the problem. If the pressure is great enough, you will go back into drugs, anger, worry, pornography, overspending, whatever it was that you used to do when you were weak.

I have known of great men, when faced with challenges in their marriages, attempted to cope with it by having an affair. Why? Their marriage was in crisis and rather than turning back to God and letting Him restore their marriage, they found comfort in someone else. If your comfort is in anything other than God, you will fail.

My relationship with Jesus is not dependent upon Belinda, my wife. It can be encouraged by her, but she does not have the power to take my faith from me. If she is weak, I can be strong and pull her up, or she can pull me up if I am weak. If we are both down, God will pull us both back up *if we will keep our eyes on Him*!

Another response your flesh will produce is apathy. *Apathy* means "to ignore a situation, believing it will go away." Things may be falling apart in your family, but you ignore it, acting like it's not there. Faith does not ignore the problem. Instead, it deals positively with the problem.

Your confidence in perilous times will remain unshaken as you put your faith in the promise of Isaiah 55:11: **So shall My Word be that goes forth from My mouth; it shall not return to Me void, but it shall accomplish what I please, and it shall prosper in the thing for which I sent it.**

Finally, Paul tells us in Hebrews 13:5,6 (AMP):

> [I will] not, [I will] not in any degree leave you helpless nor forsake nor let [you] down, (relax My hold on you). [Assuredly not]!
>
> So we take comfort and are encouraged and confidently and boldly say, The Lord is my Helper, I will not be seized with alarm [I will not fear or dread or be terrified]. What can man do to me?

Let's reprogram our thoughts to agree with God's Word. God is going to help us, and we are going to *make it*! No MAN can stop it!

4
Staying Strong in Crisis

When dealing with crisis times there are both natural and supernatural steps we take to overcome them. A big part of maintaining your strength in times of great stress and change is staying filled with the Holy Spirit. Let's look at what God's Word says:

Nehemiah 8:10 says:

> Then he said to them, "Go your way, eat the fat, drink the sweet, and send portions to those for whom nothing is prepared; for this day is holy to our LORD. Do not sorrow, for the joy of the LORD is your strength."

If the joy of the Lord is our strength, then it is obvious that many Christians are without strength. If God was not able to give you joy under adverse circumstances then it is unfair for Him to say that His joy would be your strength. We would have a fair-weather religion that only worked in ideal circumstances. Neither you nor I really believe that, even though we act that way sometimes. The first thing we must do to get through critical times is to lean on the Holy Spirit and allow Him to give us supernatural joy!

Galatians 5:22,23 says:

> But the fruit of the Spirit is love, joy, peace, longsuffering, kindness, goodness, faithfulness, gentleness, self-control. Against such there is no law.

Our spirit, through the aid of the Holy Spirit, can provide joy independent of the circumstances. Notice, there is no law against the fruit of the Spirit in our lives.

Sometimes I believe people think that the fruit of the Spirit only occurs under ideal circumstances. But if it is supernatural and it is God at work in your spirit, then it will work under all conditions.

Can you imagine God losing His joy as He looks down on earth and sees the work of the devil? He says to an angel, "Go get me an aspirin, I have a terrible headache. What am I going to do?" No, this will never occur! The reason that it will never occur is that God keeps in mind that He has already defeated the devil on the cross of Calvary and there is nothing that Satan can do to stop His plan from being accomplished on the earth.

Ask the Holy Spirit right now to fill you with His joy! That's right, defy the circumstances and rely on the power of God to give you supernatural strength in the midst of the storm! He will fill you with joy! It will become a life force in you, removing the stress that fear and depression have caused you! This life force will spring up in you as you yield to the Holy Spirit!

The prophet Isaiah tells us in Isaiah 12:2-6 about these wells! Let's look at it now:

> **Behold, God is my salvation, I will trust and not be afraid; "For YAH, the LORD, is my strength and song; He also has become my salvation."**
> **Therefore with joy you will draw water from the wells of salvation.**
> **And in that day you will say: "Praise the LORD, call upon His name; declare His deeds among the peoples, make mention that His name is exalted.**
> **"Sing to the LORD, for He has done excellent things; this is known in all the earth.**
> **"Cry out and shout, O inhabitant of Zion, for great is the Holy One of Israel in your midst!"**

We also see in the New Testament a picture of this life flow of the Holy Spirit coming out of our hearts. Jesus told us to expect a flow of life producing water out of our hearts.

Jesus said in John 7:37-39:

> On the last day, that great day of the feast, Jesus stood and cried out, saying, "If anyone thirsts, let him come to Me and drink.
>
> "He who believes in Me, as the Scripture has said, out of his heart will flow rivers of living water."
>
> But this He spoke concerning the Spirit, whom those believing in Him would receive; for the Holy Spirit was not yet given, because Jesus was not yet glorified.

Have you ever seen how happy people are around a new born baby? Life produces joy! People smile, laugh, act like babies themselves by making silly faces and noises. I even heard a few fathers shout out the news that they had a baby! Contrast that with a funeral. Usually no one is laughing. They are sad and cry. Many Christians act like funerals. They are sad! Why are they so sad? Because they are grieving over dead expectations! They don't believe they are going to make it! They appear to have more confidence that the devil's plans are going to work out rather than God's plan for their life. Even in tragedy we can recover a sense of joy knowing that God is able to turn it around! Isaiah prophesied that Jesus would have the anointing to turn impossible situations around!

Here's what he said in Isaiah 61:1-4:

> The Spirit of the Lord GOD is upon Me, because the LORD has anointed Me to preach good tidings to the poor; He has sent Me to heal the brokenhearted, to proclaim liberty to the captives, and the opening of the prison to those who are bound;
>
> To proclaim the acceptable year of the LORD, and the day of vengeance of our God; to comfort all who mourn,
>
> To console those who mourn in Zion, to give them beauty for ashes, the oil of joy for mourning, the garment of praise for the spirit of heaviness; that they

may be called trees of righteousness, the planting of the LORD, that He may be glorified.

And they shall rebuild the old ruins, they shall raise up the former desolations, and they shall repair the ruined cities, the desolations of many generations.

Jesus is in the business of healing the brokenhearted and giving us the oil of joy (oil is a type of the Holy Spirit). In other words the Holy Spirit will restore joy to the brokenhearted! He does this supernaturally! It is super "above" the natural! It is the power of God working for us! We are supposed to be happy! We have been given the Holy Spirit! He is a life flow in our hearts! He is the source of our supply! We can laugh at the future, because the future is bright!

We must learn to make our request with joy! In Philippians 1:4 Paul says, **Always in every prayer of mine making request for you all with joy.** This is a big key to maintaining joy under pressure! If you really believe that the Lord is answering your prayers, then no matter what the circumstances are, you will have a confidence and a joy that everything is going to work out all right. If God is not concerned about it, then neither am I! I recall someone saying, "If it is all right with God, then it is all right with me!"

Since the Holy Spirit, Who is God, is at work in you as well as in the circumstances, is not concerned about the outcome, then neither should we be concerned. After all, prayer is really our turning over our problem to our God and relying on His ability to work things out. The result of this confidence is a joy *unspeakable* and full of glory! Trials and tests only prove what we believe is real and the one we believe in is real!

Since our confidence is in God's Word, let's look at 1 Peter 1:3-9 and see what God says!

> Blessed be the God and Father of our Lord Jesus Christ, who according to His abundant mercy has begotten us again to a living hope through the resurrection of Jesus Christ from the dead,
>
> To an inheritance incorruptible and undefiled and that does not fade away, reserved in heaven for you,
>
> Who are kept by the power of God through faith for salvation ready to be revealed in the last time.
>
> In this you greatly rejoice, though now for a little while, if need be, you have been grieved by various trials,
>
> That the genuineness of your faith, being much more precious than gold that perishes, though it is tested by fire, may be found to praise, honor, and glory at the revelation of Jesus Christ,
>
> Whom having not seen you love. Though now you do not see Him, yet believing, you rejoice with joy inexpressible and full of glory,
>
> Receiving the end of your faith — the salvation of your souls.

Do you see it? Because we are kept by the power of God through faith (verse 5), we are able to greatly rejoice in verse 6! Most of the time we focus on the trial, but here Paul is focusing on the fact that His faith will keep him until the answer arrives and so he maintains his joy and confidence in God. This joy is hard to put into words at times! He just laughed at the circumstances and encouraged his own heart! As a result of his confidence, he received an end to his faith! Faith has an end when you receive what you have been believing for! If faith has an end, then your crisis has a positive end when you receive what you have been believing God for!

Ask God right now to help you through your difficult time! Then out loud, begin to laugh at Satan's attempts to stop you from getting your answer! That's right, laugh! You say, "I don't feel like it." Well, we are not walking by how we feel, but by what we know! If we know that everything is going to be all right, we can laugh! Just start laughing by faith, just like you were saved by faith, or even talked in tongues by faith! Step out and let that river of joy come out of your spirit!

Keep laughing until it becomes a river in you! That's right, ha ha ha ha ha ha ha ha ha.......! You ask, "What good will that do me?"

Well, let's look at what God says it will do in Psalm 126:1-3:

> **When the LORD brought back the captivity of Zion, we were like those who dream.**
>
> **Then our mouth was filled with laughter, and our tongue with singing. Then they said among the nations, "The LORD has done great things for them."**
>
> **The LORD has done great things for us, and we are glad.**

Notice, we are able to laugh because God is doing great things for us! He also says in Proverbs 17:22, **A merry heart does good like medicine, but a broken spirit dries the bones.**

A merry heart is a joyful heart, a heart filled with laughter! You see, laughing in the face of terrible circumstances only proves how much confidence you have in God's ability to work it all out! You're going to make it!

We are not just going to laugh, but we will gain strength back. Observe how Jesus handled crisis times and people in crisis. Also observe some simple but powerful things you can do to begin to get out of the crisis you are in and be stronger than when you first entered it!

5

How Jesus Handled Crisis — Managing a Crisis

In order to keep a crisis from becoming destructive, Jesus, for the joy that was set before Him endured, focusing on the solution or the outcome! He realized crisis can be a turning point for good. The primary hindrance to solving a problem and the development of a crisis is emotions getting out of control. When this happens, we should move from the crisis, which is emotionally charged, to trying to take positive steps to solve the problem. Jesus will help us do this. He is the ultimate problem-solver! He brings us peace in the midst of the storm. (Mark 4:39.)

Look for a divine response to every situation. Romans 11:4 says, **But what does the divine response say to him?** In other words, how does God want me to react rather than, how do I feel like reacting!

Here are ten principles involved in how Jesus dealt with those in crisis situations. He is our example to follow.

1. *Jesus felt compassion for the people in crisis.* Many accounts in Scripture reveal Jesus' compassion in times of crisis. It was a time of crisis for the woman who was caught in adultery when her accusers brought her to Jesus to be stoned to death. Let's look at this account in John 8:3-12:

> Then the scribes and Pharisees brought to Him [Jesus] a woman caught in adultery. And when they had set her in the midst,
> They said to Him, "Teacher, this woman was caught in adultery, in the very act.

"Now Moses, in the law, commanded us that such should be stoned. But what do You say?"

This they said, testing Him, that they might have something of which to accuse Him. But Jesus stooped down and wrote on the ground with His finger, as though He did not hear.

So when they continued asking Him, He raised Himself up and said to them, "He who is without sin among you, let him throw a stone at her first."

And again He stooped down and wrote on the ground.

Then those who heard it, being convicted by their conscience, went out one by one, beginning with the oldest even to the last. And Jesus was left alone, and the woman standing in the midst.

When Jesus had raised Himself up and saw no one but the woman, He said to her, "Woman, where are those accusers of yours? Has no one condemned you?"

She said, "No one, Lord." And Jesus said to her, "Neither do I condemn you; go and sin no more."

Then Jesus spoke to them again, saying, "I am the light of the world. He who follows Me shall not walk in darkness, but have the light of life."

The compassion of Jesus caused an exchange of the woman's sin for His righteousness! He solved the real problem! He will do the same for you in your crisis.

2. *Jesus accepted people where they were.* Jesus didn't expect people to change *before* they came to Him. Many people stop turning to God when they are under pressure and say, "I will get my life straightened out. Then I will go back to church. I will get things together, and then I will go back. I am too embarrassed to go to church because I've got a problem."

Jesus will accept you right where you are. He won't accept the condition you are in forever, but He will accept you as a person right where you are. He wants to lift you up. Once you believe He loves you, you will begin to have hope that you will make it! Jesus sees you beyond your circumstances. He sees you as you will become. So let Him help you.

3. Though Jesus preached to the masses, He focused on individual needs. God never loses sight of you as an individual. The size of the crowd does not determine whether God sees you or not, or how important you are to Him.

I have over 1,500 people in my church right now. It is possible as a Pastor to get group mentality if you're not careful. Jesus always keeps me focused on the needs of the individuals in our church. You can get lost in a church of 100 just as easily as you can in a church of a few thousand. The good news is, God never takes His eyes off you.

> What man of you, having a hundred sheep, if he loses one of them, does not leave the ninety-nine in the wilderness, and go after the one which is lost until he finds it?
>
> And when he has found it, he lays it on his shoulders, rejoicing.
>
> And when he comes home, he calls together his friends and neighbors, saying to them, "Rejoice with me, for I have found my sheep which was lost!"
>
> Luke 15:4-6

Remember, He's looking for you! He wants you to make it! Even today! How? Through the development of a relationship with Him in prayer and in the Word. Your Pastor wants you to make it too! Don't make it difficult for him to find you! Go to Him!

4. Jesus always spoke to the real need. Jesus "cut through the mustard" real quick. The real issue with the woman caught in adultery was sin! When Jesus dealt with the sin problem, the other problems also ceased! Focus on the real need. Be honest with yourself and with God!

5. ***Jesus focused on right behavior.*** In John 13, Jesus gave His disciples an example of right behavior in serving one another.

> So when He had washed their feet, taken His garments, and sat down again, He said to them, "Do you know what I have done to you?
>
> "You call Me Teacher and Lord, and you say well, for so I am.
>
> "If I then, your Lord and Teacher, have washed your feet, you also ought to wash one another's feet.
>
> *"For I have given you an example, that you should do as I have done to you.*
>
> "Most assuredly, I say to you, a servant is not greater than his master; nor is he who is sent greater than he who sent him.
>
> "If you know these things, blessed are you if you do them."
>
> **Verses 12-17**

Remember, God not only requires right behavior, but He will give you the power to change. It would be unfair of God to require of you what He is unable to help you *accomplish*! Rely on Him. Ask Him for strength to fulfill His will.

6. ***Jesus encouraged people to accept personal responsibility.*** The number one problem with our society today is people do not want to assume responsibility for what has gone wrong in their lives. Instead, they blame their problems on everybody else. Notice, those that wanted to stone the woman in adultery were eager to point out her problems without dealing with their own.

My dad and mom did the very best they could to raise me right. One of the things that showed them that Ron Clark was growing up was when I stopped blaming other people for my problems.

It doesn't take a hero to assume responsibility when something good happens, but it takes courage to assume responsibility and say, "I was wrong" when a situation merits that response. Assuming responsibility for your actions is required. If you don't, things will not improve.

7. Jesus reshaped the way people thought. To change wrong thinking, you must stop majoring on minors and stop focusing on something other than the real problem.

Look how Jesus goes straight to the problem when dealing with Peter. Matthew 16:21-23:

> From that time Jesus began to show to His disciples that He must go the Jerusalem, and suffer many things from the elders and chief priests and scribes, and be killed, and be raised the third day.
>
> Then Peter took Him aside and began to rebuke Him, saying, "Far be it from You, Lord; this shall not happen to You!"
>
> But He turned and said to Peter, "Get behind Me, Satan! You are an offense to Me, for you are not mindful of the things of God, but the things of men."

Some may say Jesus was harsh with Peter, that Peter was only concerned for the Lord's well-being. Jesus went beyond Peter's words to the real problem. Peter's real problem was that he was more mindful of the things of men than the things of God. Jesus discerned Peter's real problem. People get uncomfortable when you allow the Holy Spirit to "nail them." This is what you call pastoring people supernaturally.

> For I know the thoughts that I think toward you, says the Lord, thoughts of peace and not of evil, to give you a future and a hope.
>
> Jeremiah 29:11

When people come in for counseling with me, they want to start out with a general problem. They just beat around the bush. What is the outcome? Very little is accomplished. We make very little progress because the real issue wasn't what we talked about. Most people don't want to go very deep because they are afraid to deal with the real issue. Sometimes they want you to support their fantasy and really don't want help. Jesus wants us to focus on the real issues.

I confessed to my congregation several years ago that I had developed a bad habit of being late to everything. I asked them to forgive me because some of them had waited and waited for appointments. God was rebuilding this area. I had to stop blaming others or contrary circumstances and decide I wanted to change. My secretary reminds me now if I go five minutes late and someone is waiting because I want to be reshaped in this area. I want to break that bad habit. Change began when I was honest with myself!

8. *Jesus gave people hope.* He said, **With men this is impossible,** *but with God all things are possible* (Matt. 19:26).

I may let you down or I may not be able to solve your problem, but God can and will! There is an answer to your problem and God will help you find the answer. Ask Him. James 1:5 tells us if we lack wisdom to ask of God.

9. *Jesus encouraged people's faith.* In Matthew 8:5-10,13, Jesus praised the centurion who came to Him for the healing of his servant who was ill.

> Now when Jesus had entered Capernaum, a centurion came to Him, pleading with Him,
>
> Saying, "Lord, my servant is lying at home paralyzed, dreadfully tormented."
>
> And Jesus said to him, "I will come and heal him."
>
> The centurion answered and said, "Lord, I am not worthy that You should come under my roof. But only speak a word, and my servant will be healed.
>
> "For I also am a man under authority, having soldiers under me. And I say to this one, 'Go,' and he goes; and to another, 'Come,' and he comes; and to my servant, 'Do this,' and he does it."

> When Jesus heard it, He marveled, and said to those who followed, "Assuredly, I say to you, I have not found such great faith, not even in Israel!"
>
> Then Jesus said to the centurion, "Go your way; and as you have believed, so let it be done for you." And his servant was healed that same hour.

The centurion believed in the power and ability of Jesus to heal his servant with the Word spoken from His mouth! Jesus called him a man of "great faith." I'm sure that encouraged and strengthened the centurion's faith. This unsaved Roman had more faith than the religious people did.

10. *Jesus imparted real peace.* Sometimes circumstances don't change as fast as we want them to change. Although it takes time for things to work out, you can have peace while you are waiting.

Jesus said:

> Come to Me, all you who labor and are heavy laden, and I will give you rest.
>
> Take My yoke upon you and learn from Me, for I am gentle and lowly in heart, and you will find rest for your souls.
>
> For My yoke is easy and My burden is light.
> **Matthew 11:28-30**

Jesus also said:

> Peace I leave with you, My peace I give to you; not as the world gives do I give to you. Let not your heart be troubled, neither let it be afraid.
> **John 14:27**

Remember, peace is the *umpire* in your hearts. Begin to react to peace and not to the pressure of contrary circumstances.

6
Crisis Checklist

Here are a few strategic guidelines for successfully handling any crisis.

1. *Relax and don't allow the circumstances to control you.*

Dr. Roy Hicks, Sr., a father of faith and a dear friend who has walked the walk of faith for more than 57 years, called me during a time of great stress several years ago. He told me, "I want to give you four simple things to do when you are under pressure: 1) Talk slower; 2) Walk slower; 3) Meditate more; and 4) Sit longer." The first step to controlling circumstances is learning to control yourself.

2. *Pray and ask God what you are to do.*

James 1:5 says, **If any of you lacks wisdom, let him ask of God, who gives to all liberally and without reproach, and it will be given to him.** Too often we ask God for counsel at the end of a crisis when much of the damage is done rather than at the beginning. If He doesn't answer us fast enough with what we are to do, we start walking, talking and thinking so fast that we miss His counsel. As a result, we stay in a crisis much longer than we should.

3. *Put the crisis into the context of the big picture.*

What is this situation going to mean fifteen years from now? Don't make the crisis any bigger than it is. I'm not saying what you are going through is not a problem or it doesn't have to be dealt with, but put it in context.

The way to put it in context is to ask yourself, "Is this crisis going to bother me when I get to heaven?" If not, then it's not an eternal problem. Or, "What is the impact 1, 2, 5, 10, 20, 30 years from now?" As you can see, the impact of even the biggest trials diminish over time if you handle them right. If you don't handle them right, you could take them to the judgment seat with you and stand before God and He will ask, "Why did you leave Me? How come you turned your back on Me? Now you've got into a big problem, and that problem took your love away from Me."

Deal with the challenge in the context of the *big picture*.

4. *Get the Facts.* Are you overreacting or under-reacting? Both extremes can be costly. Some of the greatest stress I have is when I react to the wrong information. Incomplete, inaccurate, or exaggerated information will cause you to reach the wrong conclusion.

5. *Turn the sensational into simple truth.* There is a tendency to make a problem bigger than it really is, especially if we view it as bigger than what God can solve. Ask yourself, "What is the real issue?"

When Belinda and I face a problem and we cut through all the emotion and identify the real problem, we solve our challenges much more quickly.

I returned home from a trip, and Amanda, my four-year-old daughter, threw tantrum after tantrum! We exhausted ourselves trying to help her. Then we finally figured out the problem. She wanted to sit on my lap. That's all she wanted. She missed her Daddy and needed her Dad to hold her, kiss her and make her feel secure. (By the way, Belinda requires the same kind of treatment!) When Belinda and I went on the next trip, as soon as we landed at the airport, I let Amanda sit on my lap, put her arms around me, kiss me and she laid her head on my chest. We did that for five minutes. After that she was happy as a June bug on a summer day!

Sometimes the problem isn't big, but it gets out of proportion when emotions are involved.

Crisis Checklist

6. ***Do you sense any hidden agendas?*** Are people pushing for quick decisions? Does the crisis demand immediate change? What is the source of the emotional fuel that continues to aggravate it? When the hot coal is removed, the fire will go out. Only in extreme cases should you react to pressure. I still find it works out better to react to what God says.

7. ***Move away from a negative, defensive attitude to one of confidence and faith concerning the future.*** Belinda says that when I am defensive, I am usually wrong. I may not be wrong, but my direction is wrong. Move to a positive attitude about the situation you are facing. Remember, the Scripture in 2 Corinthians 9:8 says, **And God is able to make all grace abound toward you, that you, always having all sufficiency in all things, may have an abundance for every good work.**

8. ***Get a vision of what the future will be like after the crisis is solved.*** See your family in harmony, sickness gone, new job, kids happy, sin gone, your husband attending church or whatever the problem is, solved. And everything going right. Proverbs 29:18 tells us, **Where there is no vision, the people perish.** (KJV) (Vision is a mental picture of a future state.)

9. ***Establish the steps you need to take to solve the crisis.*** It's foolish not to ask for help. If you don't, you only hinder yourself. Who should you ask? People who have the victory and who know how to help you get the victory. Start listing what you need to do first. If you can't make the list of steps, then seek God for help. If you can't hear God because of turmoil, then ask yourself, "Do I need to get outside help?" James said in 1:5, **If any of you lacks wisdom, let him ask of God, who gives to all liberally and without reproach, and it will be given to him.**

10. ***Have you taken time to let the decision you have made settle in your spirit and in your mind before you act?*** Unless it is an extreme emergency, like saving the life of a

loved one or pulling someone out from in front of a car, sit on it for a few minutes. When you've got a big decision to make, wait a day or so. If you can't wait a day, wait an hour. See if it still feels good in your heart, then act! Remember, God leads you, but Satan pushes! If you feel pushed, it's probably wrong.

Pulling a child from a pool is a crisis you don't have to pray about. Unless life is threatened at that very second, tell those putting pressure on you, "I am going to spend a few minutes alone with God and get peace from Him about the decision." Then do it.

11. *Ask yourself, Would you make this same decision if the pressure was off?* If not, then don't do it. Do what you think you would do without the pressure. That's usually the best decision. Is the solution truly appropriate for the situation, or are you shooting at a hummingbird with an elephant gun? That means overreacting and doing an overkill on the problem! Are you hunting an elephant with a peashooter? That means you are underreacting and need to do more!

12. *After you decide what you are going to do, do you still feel good about it?* Isaiah 55:12 says **For you shall go out with joy, and be led out with peace.** Do only what you have peace about. Belinda and I have an agreement, we only do what *we both* have a peace about doing. The worst decisions of my life have been made when I had no peace!

13. *What is the best timing to confront the problem?* Ecclesiastes 3:1 says, **To everything there is a season, a time for every purpose under heaven.** If a crisis demands confrontation, choose a time when those involved are fresh and rested. You set the time!

14. *Now do it! Go ahead and confront the crisis.* After you have passed the above steps, do it! Take your step of faith and get out of the boat! The cost of ignoring a challenge is greater than the cost of dealing with it.

7
Assuming Personal Responsibility

> Can the Ethiopian change his skin or the leopard its spots? Then may you also do good who are accustomed to do evil.
>
> **Jeremiah 13:23**

Accustomed means "a habit that is contracted by long practice, or learned behavior." In other words, people feel like they can't change. Jeremiah said, **Can the Ethiopian change his skin or the leopard its spots?** It's impossible. Many people feel it's just as impossible to change bad habits.

I've seen people who try to lose weight experience frustrations. They will lose a little bit and then gain it all back. It reinforces in them, "I can't change." Every time they diet and go back to excessive eating habits, they say, "It is impossible to lose weight." Our entire society is built on impossibilities or a mentality of "learn to live with it."

With faith in God, all things are possible. To walk in faith you must assume responsibility for your actions. It is hard to start walking a life of faith after years of practicing doubt and unbelief. You are responsible for your actions of faith or doubt. Some people have said to me, "Pastor, the message of faith is too hard." My response is, "It is as hard as changing the spots on a leopard if you don't have faith in God." Responsibility means that we are required to respond to "His" ability, not our own.

We're talking about lifelong habits, and without God's ability many will not change. Unbelief is a habit. To change it is difficult. Anyone who tells you that change is easy is not from our planet! Change is difficult because, 1) Some Christians are unwilling to change; 2) They don't know how to change; and 3) They don't want to assume the personal responsibility that is necessary for change to occur.

Of the people who come to my church, I would say that about 99 percent of them want to change, but many don't know how to change. Some people say, "That's just the way I am." Why don't we say, "That's just the way I was"? Or we say, "I'll never change. I was born this way." Have you ever heard someone justify their anger by saying, "I am Irish"? Or they justify their impatience with, "I've got Irish blood flowing in my veins." In other words, I am not responsible for my actions. Neither am I responding to "God's" ability to change my actions.

Galatians 5:22,23 says, **But the fruit of the Spirit is love, joy, peace, longsuffering, kindness, goodness, faithfulness, gentleness, self-control.**

First Timothy 6:11 says, **But you, O man of God, flee these things and pursue righteousness, godliness, faith, love, patience, gentleness.** Second Thessalonians 3:5 says, **Now may the Lord direct your hearts into the love of God and into the patience of Christ.** Colossians 1:11 says, **Strengthened with all might, according to His glorious power, for all patience and longsuffering with joy.**

What about your Irish blood? The Bible also says that life is in the blood. But after Adam sinned, sin was passed down from the blood of Adam, so everyone is dealing with the sin nature. God has the power to deliver you from anger, because the power of God is greater than the power of sin. Sin can be overcome, which means the power that is in you as a Christian is greater than the power that is in the world of sin. Light is greater than darkness. In fact, light dispels darkness. Darkness cannot stop the light.

It's difficult to change, but it is not impossible when we rely on "His" ability. The number one reason people have trouble changing is the four-letter word, *past*. The one anchor that hooks you and keeps you from progressing in your spiritual walk is your view of the past. Change is impossible as long as you focus your attention on your past. The past does not need the change. It's the present you can do something about.

Have you ever wondered why the auto makers made the rear-view mirror smaller than your windshield? So you don't spend too much time looking back! It's hard to make real progress with all your attention towards the past!

It is just as bad to spend all your time dreaming about the future! We must deal with today. Some people ask, "But what about the future?" The person who lives only in the future is a worry wart and never deals with today. Matthew 6:25-34 teaches this truth.

> **Therefore I say to you, do not worry about your life, what you will eat or what you will drink; nor about your body, what you will put on. Is not life more than food and the body more than clothing?**
>
> **Look at the birds of the air, for they neither sow nor reap nor gather into barns; yet your heavenly Father feeds them. Are you not of more value than they?**
>
> **Which of you by worrying can add one cubit to his stature?**
>
> **So why do you worry about clothing? Consider the lilies of the field, how they grow: they neither toil nor spin;**
>
> **And yet I say to you that even Solomon in all his glory was not arrayed like one of these.**
>
> **Now if God so clothes the grass of the field, which today is, and tomorrow is thrown into the oven, will He not much more clothe you, O you of little faith?**
>
> **Therefore do not worry, saying, "What shall we eat?" or "What shall we drink?" or "What shall we wear?"**

For after all these things the Gentiles seek. For your heavenly Father knows that you need all these things.
But seek first the kingdom of God and His righteousness, and all these things shall be added to you.
Therefore do not worry about tomorrow, for tomorrow will worry about its own things. Sufficient for the day is its own trouble.

The *balanced* Christian is the one who lives in the *now* and takes responsibility for what's happening. He looks back at lessons learned and he looks to the future to where he's going, but has learned to deal with today. Scripture says, **Now faith is the substance of things hoped for, the evidence of things not seen.** (Heb. 11:1). Faith is a *now* place. It is a place that brings great balance between what has happened to you in the past and what will happen to you in the future.

Some people worry about trying to break a habit. "I'll never be able to stop doing this." My question is, "Can you stop for now? If you are a smoker, can you stop smoking right now? Have you stopped smoking, drinking, adultery, cursing and lying in the last minute?" Then you are making progress.

Thoughts that come to you from the devil or from your flesh that aren't spoken and expressed are aborted, miscarried, or stillborn. Satan wants you to think that every thought condemns you, yet Scripture says, **Beloved, if our heart does not condemn us, we have confidence toward God** (1 John 3:21).

If Satan can get you to think that you have sinned just because you thought something, then he has got you in a trap that you will never get out of. Everybody thinks thoughts that they shouldn't at times, but we don't have to put them in action!

If we want to be a balanced Christian, we've got to start living in the *now* and assume responsibility by bringing our thoughts into captivity, allowing wrong thoughts to be stillborn. When you speak wrong thoughts, you create substance. What you *say* creates substance. The universe was formed with words, and it is controlled by words. Your life is also controlled with words. You are living in the results of what you have thought and *said*!

Words can be spoken and nullified. Contracts can be made and changed or broken legally. Ask God to forgive you and begin to break the power of the words you have spoken. We must learn how to create what we want with our words and let the rest of our words die stillborn.

I could say, "I am worried my dad might die." That is dealing with tomorrow. Can I do anything about tomorrow? No, Scripture says tomorrow will worry about itself. But my dad isn't dead, so we are enjoying our times together. I can pick up the phone and call him right now because he's still living. Taking responsibility allows me to enjoy the blessings of today. I can do something about it today. But tomorrow, I may not have a chance.

Most people put off breaking bad habits until tomorrow. Tomorrow never arrives, because we live in the now. Take responsibility for today.

Have you ever heard someone make the excuse, "If the situation was different, I could change." The truth is, the only way the situation will change is if *you* change.

Let's look at 1 Peter 3 in relationship to making excuses. "Wives, be submissive to your own husbands after they are perfect...when they agree with you...only after they are saved and do everything you want them to do!" Verse 1 doesn't read that way, does it?

> **Wives, likewise, be submissive to your own husbands, that even if some do not obey the word, they, without a word, may be won by the conduct of their wives.**

To change a situation, *you* must first change. That will effect change in others. One of three things will happen if you change: 1) The situation will change; 2) Attitudes will change; or 3) Others will change.

Have you ever heard the expression, "It takes two to tango?" You can stop all fights right now if you refuse to fight. That may not cause everything to become perfect yet, but you can effect change.

Some of us have said, "I'll change when the situation changes." I am saying, we can change situations if we will first submit to God and ask Him to change us as individuals. Respond to His ability!

I had someone get upset with me because he thought I said something that I did not say. Now, I'm not making excuses for something I did say and trying to worm out of it. He thought I said something that was disrespectful to him, and he was upset with me. As soon as I found out about it, I went straight to the person and confronted him with the situation. I assumed responsibility.

I said, "I am very sorry if I have done anything that has hurt your feelings. I would never do anything to hurt you purposely. Will you forgive me?"

The person let it all come out while I sat there not saying a word. I let him get it off his chest. Then I said, "I know it's hard to believe, based upon what you've said to me, but I did not say that."

He said, "That's hard to believe." I said, "But it's the truth." So we talked for two or three more minutes. The person hugged my neck and we are buddies again, but *I had to change first*. If I had gotten defensive, we could still be at odds with each other. I didn't wait for him to make one move. If I had gone to him and he said, "I still don't believe you," it wouldn't be my problem anymore. I can't change him, I am only responsible for my actions.

You can change circumstances. If you are married to someone who isn't saved, you can change the situation by the way you act. As long as they are dictating the terms to you, they are in control, but you can change that by the way you respond. The Word tells us that we can control ourselves. As soon as I return good for evil, then I am in control. **Do not be overcome by evil, but overcome evil with good** (Rom. 12:21). If you return evil for evil, the person feels justified for his own evil actions.

Every time you obey the Word and you return good for evil, you remove yourself from the equation that produces justification in the person's life. That's what Jesus did when He died on the cross. He removed every bit of justification and every claim the devil had when He died on the cross.

Jesus said, "I can lay My life down and take it right back up again. You're not doing this to Me. I am doing it. I am going to that cross to die for those people because I love them and you can't stop Me" (my interpretation of John 10:17,18). That's a far cry from His enemies sending Him to the gallows. By apparently losing, Jesus ultimately won for everyone! Jesus was the greatest example of someone who took responsibility by responding to God's ability and the result was victory! And that victory produced change forever, for everyone who will respond.

If you desire to effect change, you must assume personal responsibility. You can't continue to blame others for your problems, even if they are 90 percent at fault! The 10 percent investment you have in the relationship is enough to create change that will cause the whole relationship to change. As soon as you say, "It will never change," it's over. But as soon as you begin to change yourself and take personal responsibility for your part, you sow a seed that will grow and produce good fruit.

First Corinthians 13:8 says, **Love never fails.** If it ever fails, God fails! The Scripture says God cannot lie (Num.

23:19; Tit. 1:2). The problem is, we fail to love. But if we work at it, it will work for us. Galatians 5:6 tells us that faith works by love. Love makes faith work, and faith makes love work. Really, all love is, is treating others the way we want to be treated!

In handling a crisis, sometimes we are like a teapot, short and stout! We begin to simmer and boil and then we have to cool down after spewing out a little spray! I do that sometimes just like you do! Then God gets a hold of me, "Are you through?"

When I hear the Holy Spirit or my mother call me "Ronald," I know it's time for whatever is going on to come to an end.

I used to get in big trouble for digging in my mother's purse. When I saw my daughter pick up my mother's purse and dump it out looking for candy, my mom laughed. I said, "That's not fair. You used to spank me over stuff like that!" My mom made a very interesting statement: "It's not my responsibility to raise your children." She said it in a very sweet way, but she said it! She also said, "I am through raising my children. I am going to spoil yours." I guess that is a grandma's prerogative.

I watched my dad let Wilson, my son, do something he shouldn't have done. I heard Belinda, "Wilson Davis!" My son froze, but my dad was laughing. My dad would say the same thing my mom said: "It's your youngster." They don't do that on everything, but for the most part they are going to spoil them real good, fill them full of sugar and then head on down the road! I have personal responsibility with my children that I can't delegate to anyone else.

No one can change you but *you*. I don't expect you to raise my children. They sit on the front row with Belinda for about thirty minutes during a service. Then they leave and go to children's church. But that's all right for four and five years of age. There will come a day when they will sit through the entire service.

Maturity occurs when you begin to assume personal responsibility and control yourself. I have met people thirty years old who are still babies because they can't control themselves. The greatest way to change any situation is for you and me to take personal responsibility for our own actions.

God wants every person to go to heaven, but if they don't make it, it won't be because of a lack of desire on God's part. It will be because of a lack of personal responsibility on their part. The Bible says God has provided everything we need for life and godliness, which means all of us have every tool available to us if we will use it. The only reason we don't use the tools we have is that we haven't taken personal responsibility to effect change in our own lives.

If you do not take personal responsibility for yourself, you require others to control you. People are mature when they can control their own behavior. I have met children twelve and fourteen years old who know how to control their own behavior. Yet, I have met other adults, some in their sixties, who still can't control their mouth, attitudes and actions.

My responsibility is to teach my children internal control so they won't need external control when they are older. Jails are full of people who never learned how to take personal responsibility for their own actions as children. They never learned self-control. Now that we are older, what we didn't learn, we can learn with God's help.

Remember when God called to Adam in the garden and asked, **Where are you?** (Gen. 3:9). God was trying to get Adam to take personal responsibility for the wrong that he had committed. Adam responded, **I heard Your voice in**

the garden, and I was afraid because I was naked; and I hid myself (Gen. 3:10). God was looking for Adam to take responsibility.

Over a process of time, God has tried to teach the human race how to become morally responsible for their actions again. Our society has made an excuse. The Dr. Spock generation made an excuse as to why we do not have to be responsible for our actions. In fact, we have come up with slogans like, "If it feels good, do it."

More than anything else, teenagers want to be respected, yet respect is not given. It is earned by being responsible.

My brother and I are two weeks apart in age. Figure that one out! We used to blow people's minds and they would say, "Your mama stayed in labor a long time." No, my mom is my stepmother. My brother got his driver's license months before I got mine. It made me mad. I remember my dad saying to me, "How can I hold David back because he is being responsible with his life and reward you when you are being irresponsible? You will earn that license." That gave me great motivation for change. Needless to say, it wasn't many months before I had made significant changes in my attitude and had my license.

When you are born again, you are a baby. A biker came into one of our services and was saved. He came up to me and said, "Pastor, that was a damn good sermon!" As carnal as it was, he didn't know any better. I said, "Thank you" and took it as a great compliment because he was a spiritual baby. One week earlier he had been selling dope. Now he has the Holy Spirit in him and the power to change! Until the previous week, he had never heard a sermon and didn't even know what it was.

That's okay out of a baby, but if church members come up to me in like manner, I am going to exercise my responsibility and authority! Why treat them different? For the same reason you expect more out of your teenager than your toddler! You expect them to grow up and learn to control themselves.

So what happens if a person doesn't mature spiritually? It's up to the pastor and those in positions of leadership to exercise their authority. I don't like it any more than I like spanking my son Wilson, or Amanda, my little daughter. If I had my way, I'd just let you and God work it out, but there are times when a pastor has to use his authority. You may be thinking, "It's voluntary authority." You are right. But you'd be an idiot to run from correction, particularly from a pastor or leader who loves you enough to tell you the truth. **Remember those who rule over you, who have spoken the word of God to you** (Heb. 13:7). Proverbs 15:10 says, **He who hates correction will die.** Learn to love correction. Not because it feels good, but because it will yield the peaceable fruit of righteousness (Heb. 12:11).

Many children and teenagers don't follow their parents because the parents aren't mature enough to receive correction for the things they have done wrong. Yet they require their children to do what they aren't willing to do themselves, even telling them, "Do as I say, not as I do!"

When you are born again, God will take you where you are and help you grow up in Him so you will require less and less control from others in your life. Remember, as you begin to take control, you are assuming responsibility and God will then respond with His ability! With God, all things are possible!

8
Breaking Bad Habits That Create Crisis!

To head off a crisis or to walk through it into victory, we need to get rid of bad habits. Many crisis situations we face are created by bad habits.

For years after I had completed high school, I continued to put on weight. I gained weight until my daughter Amanda was born, at which time I weighed 230 pounds at 6'1". I wasn't in good shape! My weight used to talk to me, "You will never get rid of me." I found my eating habits reflected a lack of self-control in my life.

I struggled until I finally acknowledged what the Bible says about bringing your body under control and came in line with it. I submitted to the authority of God's Word. I changed the way I ate and I lost nearly 60 pounds, most of which I have kept off. I had to change habits that had crept into my life and were controlling me. Submitting to authority is a key to breaking bad habits.

A couple talked to me recently about strife in their home and asked, "How do we get rid of it?" I said to the wife, "Very easy. Even if you believe your husband is wrong, agree with him." Think about it! There is no better way to put the husband in a position to lead than for the wife to say, "Okay, if that's what you want to do, let's go for it." "But what if he does something stupid?" Well, it is not the first time he has, nor will it be the last!

Oh, by the way, when is the last time you did something stupid? Did you want others to give up on you or forgive you? For there to be peace in the home, all it takes is *one person who will always agree*. (I'm not talking about situations that are illegal or immoral.) You can have a discussion and make yourself known, but once decision time comes, say to the husband, "Whatever you say." Why am I saying this? Because the Scripture teaches us that husbands should lead and take responsibility for the family! They won't if you don't cooperate.

When Belinda and I were first married, I used to buy a new car every year, even if I didn't need it, which I didn't. This obsession created a crisis in our lives. I'd lose a couple thousand dollars in the deal. After losing that amount each year for two or three consecutive years, I didn't have much left. Every year Belinda would say, "Honey, I don't think we ought to do that." I would say, "But honey, I want that new car." Belinda would just agree with me until one day I woke up. Now she has to make me go get a new car.

It doesn't take nagging to stop me now (nagging is telling someone to do something over and over when they already know they are supposed to do it). It just takes God speaking to me (often God talks to me out of my wife's counsel). When Belinda would nag, I would make excuses, but when she said, "Okay, honey, if that's what you want to do," all the pressure was on me. I became responsible because of her submission.

Even in silence, wives have great power. The worst thing a husband and wife can do is vie for the top position. Being the head does not mean that you are better, no more than the Father being the head of Jesus makes Him better than Jesus. Submission doesn't make you any less of a person. All it means is there is divine order. And we serve a God of order! Jesus said, **The Son can do nothing of Himself, but what He sees the Father do; for whatever He does, the Son also does in like manner** (John 5:19).

Breaking Bad Habits That Create Crisis!

The Holy Spirit is submitted to the Father and to the Son. He is committed to speak only what He hears the Father and the Son saying, but that does not make Him any less God.

When I was in the military, one sergeant was much smarter than the captain he served, and he always knew what to do. Yet, he always respected the captain's position with, "Yes, Sir." Just because someone ranks higher than you does not make them better, smarter, or more talented. It simply means there is order.

You may be smarter than a policeman, but if he stops you, that's not the time to get into a debate over who has more brains. In fact, the more you debate him, the more charges he may check against you. He doesn't have to prove his brilliance. He is showing you his authority, and his authority gives him the right to write you a ticket. You've got to work your situation out with him some other way than through argument.

Wives, that's the way to do it with your husband and children. If the wife is respectful to the husband in submitting to his authority, the children will begin to follow her example.

If you are waiting for the ideal condition or circumstance to submit to authority and break those bad habits, the ideal condition will never come. Only crisis after crisis will come, all of which are unnecessary. Satan will make sure of that. When you submit, situations and attitudes will change. When you change, others will change, but if you don't change, nothing changes.

Personal responsibility is absolutely essential if you are going to break free. You cannot blame your wife, your children, or your parents. You cannot blame your employer, your employees, your church, or God. The next stop in breaking bad habits is an attitude of repentance.

Look at Romans 2:4 which says, **Or do you despise the riches of His goodness, forbearance, and longsuffering, not knowing that the goodness of God leads you to repentance?** The Greek word for repentance is *metanoia*, which means "afterthought or change of mind; that which would reverse the effects of a previous state of mind; reversal of another's decision." When you repent of something, you reverse your decision.

Repentance is a call for change — a change of mind, a change of life. Repentance is a spiritual force that changes your direction! Every promise in the Bible begins with repentance. God can't save you until you repent. He can't do anything for you unless you decide to go His way.

Hebrews 12:16,17 says:

> **Lest there be any fornicator or profane person like Esau, who for one morsel of food sold his birthright.**
>
> **For you know that afterward, when he wanted to inherit the blessing, he was rejected, for he found no place for repentance, though he sought it diligently with tears.**

It is amazing to me that Adam and Eve sold eternity for a piece of fruit. It is also troubling to me to see believers who quit church because of discouragement or thinking their problems will never change.

I have met men who at one time were preaching the Gospel of Jesus Christ and serving Him with their whole heart. Now they are not going to church at all because of a habit or a problem. Why does this happen? There is no place of repentance in their lives. They failed to put confidence in the power of the Holy Spirit to produce change. To them, their problems seemed bigger than God!

Esau could have repented. Rather than repent, Esau didn't want to repent at all. His tears were tears of regret, not tears of sorrow that led to repentance.

Have you ever seen people who were caught in some kind of problem, where they wept and had a degree of brokenness, yet instead of becoming more tender, they became even harder? It's like the little boy who got his hand caught in the cookie jar. He didn't repent. He said, "I am sorry I got caught."

Second Corinthians 7:10 says, **For godly sorrow produces repentance leading to salvation, not to be regretted; but the sorrow of the world produces death.** Since repentance is a decision to go another way, godly sorrow produces a decision: "I am not going that way anymore. I am going to turn around."

The sorrow of the world is the sorrow that regrets being caught. "I'm really sorry, not that I did wrong, but that you caught me doing wrong." That doesn't produce life and change, only death and destruction. *Salvation*, as used in this verse, means "safety, preservation, deliverance, health and healing." So there is a godly sorrow that produces safety, preservation, deliverance, health and healing. Godly sorrow will get you out of trouble. It will cause the power of God to move on your behalf. It will cause that which looks impossible to turn to be a blessing in your life.

When there is true repentance, the Holy Spirit always changes you. Godly sorrow involves a decision that is irrevocable.

I've watched repentance and godly sorrow work in my children. I've seen Wilson do something wrong, get caught and give a look of, "I'm sorry I got caught." He does certain things wrong and we use a little spoon to give him a paddling. Now, the world says spanking is wrong. Rebellion automatically gets a paddling at our house. God designed this means of correction. The Scripture says in Proverbs 13:24, **He who spares his rod hates his son, but he who loves him disciplines him promptly.**

I know our modern society. They are smart and want to "improve" on the so-called backward ways of the Bible. But look at how those kids are being trained by this kind of philosophy! Juvenile delinquency is at an all time high and it's not because the parents have given these kids the discipline they need. The rest of the body is bony, except for the bottom. It is designed in such a way as to absorb shock without long-lasting problems!

One or two applications of a spoon to the backside of a child causes godly sorrow. A child may be angry because he got caught, but with one or two swats, he will repent and decide not to repeat the behavior. We only spank for rebellion, willful disobedience, or lying.

When we discipline our children, we go through a five-point plan: 1) Tell them you love them; 2) Tell them what the Bible says about what they did; 3) Tell them the reason you are going to spank is because you do not want the attitude or action to continue; 4) Give them a little paddling; and 5) Then after the crying, hug their neck and reassure them of your love. Not everything deserves a spanking, and certainly it is not an outlet for an angry parent. If you are angry, *wait* until you cool off.

When there is true repentance, the Holy Spirit can work. Acts 26:20 says, **But declared first to those in Damascus and in Jerusalem, and throughout all the region of Judea, and then to the Gentiles, that they should repent, turn to God, and do works befitting repentance.** In other words, when you repent and turn to God, a work is produced by it. There is a change in behavior.

You can deal with the past by dealing with the present guilt so the past can be buried with Christ. When you really repent, the sin is buried with Christ. When it is buried under the shed blood of Jesus Christ, God never brings it up again. Many people don't change because of their past, which constantly calls out to them, "You will never change."

God gives supernatural ability called "grace" to change. You don't have to pull yourself up by your boot straps and try to make yourself change. God will give you supernatural ability to change, so your confession can be, "I used to smoke, but by God's grace, I will never smoke again." That's true repentance which will lead to change.

Colossians 2:12 says, **Buried with Him in baptism, in which you also were raised with Him through faith in the working of God, who raised Him from the dead.** It's the power of God that raised Jesus from the dead. Scripture says this is the same power that quickens our mortal bodies. God will produce change in you with His power and His Spirit.

When I brought my appetite under control by saying, "no" to my flesh, my thought life began to line up with the Word. I tell my body, "You are not running the show, man. I am going to live to be ninety." My cholesterol level was blowing the top out, I had high blood pressure and the doctor was getting ready to put me on medicine when I was at 230 pounds. Now, my blood pressure and heart rate are all normal. Although I get the benefit out of this change, God is the One Who helped me.

I got so brave after losing weight that I had all my trousers taken in! That was faith! I've heard people say, "If you ever gain it back, you will be bigger than you were before." Not this man! I am agreeing with what God says. He says I can have what I say, and I am saying that I am not gaining that weight back. I have built new eating habits, and I am sticking with it.

Someone says, "But I saw you have a piece of pie." I'm not saying I can't have pie, but the pie can't have me! Occasionally, I will eat a little piece of dessert. I love to eat a small piece and then say to my body, "You can't have anymore."

You can win in the battle you are facing. Your spirit man wants to keep things under control, but your body must be brought into submission to God.

> **I beseech you therefore, brethren, by the mercies of God, that you present your bodies a living sacrifice, holy, acceptable to God, which is your reasonable service.**
> **Romans 12:1**

Philippians 3:13,14 says:

> **Brethren, I do not count myself to have apprehended** [that means I haven't arrived]; **but one thing I do, forgetting those things which are behind and reaching forward to those things which are ahead,**
>
> **I press toward the goal for the prize of the upward call of God in Christ Jesus.**

To break bad habits you must forget the things which are behind and press toward your new position in Christ. That means old habits are no longer an issue and you don't talk about them anymore. You can find out if you've done it by the way you talk. Do you talk as if your old man is still alive, or do you talk as if he's in the grave?

When my grandpa was alive, I referred to him in a different way than I do now because he has gone on to be with the Lord. The Bible says your old man is dead when you are born again. If the old man is dead, then talk about him as if you've already had the funeral. Don't talk about him as if he's still alive. Part of the problem is, we have let the old man live. We resurrect him.

Paul says, **I have been crucified with Christ; it is no longer I who live, but Christ lives in me; and the life which I now live in the flesh I live by faith in the Son of God, who loved me and gave Himself for me** (Gal. 2:20).

That old stinking man that did whatever he wanted to do has died. I am a new man. I do what God wants me to do. That should be your confession, because confession brings possession.

Have you ever taken a big piece of chocolate cake with thick icing and a big scoop of double-fudge ice cream to the graveyard and laid it out there? If a dog or a raccoon doesn't get it, that thing will still be there the next morning. Now, I'm sure there are people in the graveyard who used to be controlled by chocolate. But you can buy the biggest hunk of chocolate and put it next to their grave, and when you wake up the next day, that little piece of chocolate will still be there.

Some of those in the graveyard were controlled by lust, but you can buy five hundred pornographic magazines, place them on top of the grave, and when you go there the next day, none of them will have been read. Why? Because a dead man doesn't move! Because you are dead to sin and alive to God, when a temptation comes to you, you need to say, "I am dead to that."

When I go to a convenience store and walk by the beer case, I don't stop and say, "I haven't seen cans like that" and start dwelling on it. I died to drinking many years ago. I'm dead to that. It's not only I can't have it, but I don't want it. My "dead man" isn't thirsty for beer.

If our old man is dead, we need to act like it by doing what is right. When is a liar no longer a liar? When he becomes a *truth-teller*, not when he stops lying. If you just stop lying, all you are doing is waiting for another opportunity to lie. But when you begin to say the truth, then you become a truth-teller. You have a choice between telling what is true and what is false. The way to break the habit of lying is by telling the truth.

Ephesians 4:25 says, **Therefore, putting away lying, let each one speak truth with his neighbor, for we are members of one another.**

So how do you change? Put off the old nature and then put on the new man.

> That you *put off*, concerning your former conduct, the old man which grows corrupt according to the deceitful lusts,
> And be renewed in the spirit of your mind,
> And that you *put on* the new man which was created according to God, in true righteousness and holiness.
>
> Ephesians 4:22-24

To put off and put on is a choice, similar to the advice Dr. Roy Hicks, Sr. gave me regarding stress: walk slower, talk slower, sit longer and meditate more. It works. It has helped me gain control of my emotions in many situations.

Ephesians 4:1-7 says:

> **I, therefore, the prisoner of the Lord** [many people in the Body of Christ are prisoners to a lot of things], **beseech you to walk worthy of the calling with which you were called,**
> **With all lowliness and gentleness, with longsuffering, bearing with one another in love,**
> **Endeavoring to keep the unity of the Spirit in the bond of peace.**
> **There is one body and one Spirit, just as you were called in one hope of your calling;**
> **One Lord, one faith, one baptism;**
> **One God and Father of all, who is above all, and through all, and in you all.**
> **But to each one of us grace was given according to the measure of Christ's gift.**

Grace is divine enablement or ability to do whatever God has required of you. He will never ask you to do what you cannot do.

Paul continues:

> Therefore He says: "When He ascended on high, He led captivity captive, and gave gifts to men."
> (Now this, "He ascended" — what does it mean but that He also first descended into the lower parts of the earth?

> He who descended is also the One who ascended far above all the heavens, that He might fill all things.)
>
> And He Himself gave some to be apostles, some prophets, some evangelists, some pastors and teachers,
>
> For the equipping of the saints for the work of the ministry, for the edifying of the body of Christ,
>
> Till we all come to the unity of the faith and the knowledge of the Son of God, to a perfect man, to the measure of the stature of the fullness of Christ;
>
> That we should no longer be children, tossed to and fro and carried about with every wind of doctrine, by the trickery of men, in the cunning craftiness of deceitful plotting,
>
> But, speaking the truth in love, may grow up in all things into Him who is the head — Christ —
>
> From whom the whole body, joined and knit together by what every joint supplies, according to the effective working by which every part does its share, causes growth of the body for the edifying of itself in love.
>
> This I say, therefore, and testify in the Lord, that you should no longer walk as the rest of the Gentiles walk, in the futility of their mind.
>
> **Ephesians 4:8-17**

Gentiles, unbelievers, or people outside of Christ, are often bound by habits. If you have unsaved loved ones, stop trying to make them change from the outside in. They have no idea what you are talking about when you say to abstain from evil. Many of them are bound by wrong habits, and it is unfair of you to require them to walk like you walk when you've got the help of God. We need to pray for them to be changed from the inside out, not from the outside in. You can control a man, but you can't change him except with the help of God.

> Having their understanding darkened, being alienated from the life of God, because of the ignorance that is in them, because of the blindness of their heart.
>
> **Ephesians 4:18**

You are no longer ignorant when the Holy Ghost lives in you. You have the mind of Christ as you renew your mind with the Word of God, and with God's help you can do anything He asks you to do. Paul said, **I can do all things through Christ who strengthens me** (Phil. 4:13).

Ignorance produces a hard heart. You can identify an ignoramus by the hardness of his or her heart. The harder the heart, the dumber the person, to the point where the person shakes his or her fist in the face of God, as if He was the problem. That's ignorance gone to seed, and the seed is springing up into full bloom!

> **Who, being past feeling, have given themselves over to lewdness, to work all uncleanness with greediness.**
>
> **But you have not so learned Christ,**
>
> **If indeed you have heard Him and have been taught by Him, as the truth is in Jesus:**
>
> **That you *put off*, concerning your former conduct, the old man which grows corrupt according to the deceitful lusts,**
>
> **And be renewed in the spirit of your mind,**
>
> **And that you *put on* the new man.**
>
> **Ephesians 4:19-24**

The beginning of the breakdown of bad habits in your life is when you put off the old and put on the new nature. Paul says to put off concerning your former conduct. Anything that is one second ago is "former." You may be thinking, "I repent of a bad habit, go half a day and I do it again." It was only a habit for a second, you repented and then it became a "former habit." This avoids a crisis!

Where does faith live? *Now* **faith is** (Hebrews 11:1). *Now* is where you live. You say, "But I cussed yesterday." Did you cuss today? Thank God, it is a "former habit." That's truth and reality.

> That you put off, concerning your former conduct, the old man which grows corrupt according to the deceitful lusts.
>
> **Ephesians 4:22**

Your life grows corrupt according to deceitful lusts. In other words, your old man begins to convince you that you cannot change.

I have had people say to me, "I am trying to break this bad habit, and the thoughts keep coming to me, so I think, 'God, You are unhappy with me because those thoughts came to me. I might as well give in.'"

All of us have probably thought that way at times, because the devil tries to convince us that the wrong thoughts that come are sin. Even Jesus was tempted, but it is how we respond to the thoughts that cause them to be sin or not. What you *say* locates you, not what you think.

Paul said:

> And be renewed in the spirit of your mind,
>
> And that you put on the new man which was created according to God, in true righteousness and holiness.
>
> **Ephesians 4:23,24**

The creation of the new man has already occurred.

> Therefore, putting away lying, let each one of you speak truth with his neighbor, for we are members of one another.
>
> Be angry, and do not sin: do not let the sun go down on your wrath,
>
> Nor give place to the devil.
>
> **Ephesians 4:25-27**

For years I was convinced that I'd never be able to control my thoughts. But I learned, as long as I didn't speak them, I was in control. When you speak your bad thoughts, you are no longer in control. They are in control of you. As soon as you speak negative thoughts, you are in bondage.

Casting Down Imaginations and Arguments

Second Corinthians 10:1-5 says:

> Now I, Paul, myself am pleading with you by the meekness and gentleness of Christ — who in presence am lowly among you, but being absent am bold toward you.
>
> But I beg you that when I am present I may not be bold with that confidence by which I intend to be bold against some, who think of us as if we walked according to the flesh.
>
> For though we walk in the flesh, we do not war according to the flesh.
>
> For the weapons of our warfare are not carnal [they are not of the flesh] **but mighty in God for pulling down strongholds,**
>
> **Casting down arguments** [or imaginations] **and every high thing that exalts itself against the knowledge of God, bringing every thought into captivity to the obedience of Christ.**

Where do the arguments and imaginations occur? In your little old mind! Where do they get cast down from? Your mind. How do you cast them down? Don't speak them, because thoughts left unspoken die.

We are to speak what God says. Every time a temptation comes that says, "You can't," speak a word which says *you can*. Not only will the thought die in your mind, but you can replace it with good thoughts that will grow and bring forth good fruit.

Verse 5 in the King James Version says:

> **Casting down imaginations, and every high thing that exalteth itself against the knowledge of God, and bringing into captivity every thought to the obedience of Christ.**

The knowledge of God is the Word of God. Put everything down that argues with the Word. In other words, if it doesn't agree with the Word, don't speak it.

James 5:14,15 says:

> **Is anyone among you sick? Let him call for the elders of the church, and let them pray over him, anointing him with oil in the name of the Lord.**
>
> **And the prayer of faith will save the sick, and the Lord will raise him up. And if he has committed sins, he will be forgiven.**

Once you have been prayed for and pain hits you, it communicates to your brain, "The prayer didn't work." That's an imagination because it does not agree with the Word, and it begins to grow with, "What if?" The "What if" devil is the biggest devil of all. "What if it didn't work? What if I don't get healed? What if? What if? What if? What if enough money doesn't come in? What if we don't get our new building? What if the landlord comes tomorrow and locks the door? What if we are out in the street and we don't even have our chairs anymore and we have to sit on the ground?"

If you don't cast down those thoughts, replacing them with God's promises, you will "What if" yourself right into the biggest mess and then begin to speak it. As you speak it, you begin to create on the outside what you have created on the inside with your own words. An imagination builds an image of a future state. With your words, begin to build inside of you what is going to happen according to God's Word.

Long before a marriage splits, imaginations are built that the marriage won't work. Imaginations, when meditated upon and spoken out, create your own future, whether good or bad.

Mark 11:22 says, **So Jesus answered and said to them, "Have faith in God."** In other words, have the God-kind of faith or have *now* faith.

> **For assuredly, I say to you, whoever says to this mountain, "Be removed and be cast into the sea," and does not doubt in his heart, but believes that those things which he says will be done, he will have whatever he *says*.**
>
> Mark 11:23

He will have whatever he thinks? Whatever he imagines? No, as long as it is an imagination, it will die unborn if it isn't expressed in words. You kill evil or negative imaginations by speaking what God's Word says about you.

The devil comes to you and says, "Your husband is never going to change. Your finances will never change. Your life is never going to change. Nothing is ever going to change. Look at you. You can't even stop eating chocolate. You can't even stop getting angry at little things. How are you going to stop something as big as this? You might as well give up." This is how Satan builds an imagination.

He keeps it up. "Your husband has been mean to you all these years. He is never going to stop being mean to you. In fact, he is always going to be mean to you. Your boss is never going to change. You might as well quit." These kinds of thoughts give you a mental picture of failure if they aren't stopped with what God's Word says about you. All of this leads to unnecessary crisis. Instead of killing the thought of failure with God's Word, some people have resigned themselves to defeat. "We might as well get a divorce."

I have had couples tell me, "The first time the D word (divorce) came out of my mouth, it was like a dagger stuck in both of us." That D word is a powerful word. It creates a mental picture of total failure, and unless it is repented of, causing a turning around, the failure picture will continue to grow until divorce becomes a reality.

The D word was buried with Jesus at Calvary. You can choose to abort failure by changing your words and behavior. Even if your mate hasn't changed, he or she will see the positive change in you and will be affected by it.

Begin to confess, "I can do all things through Christ Who strengthens me." Keep confessing it until you build a mental picture of succeeding in whatever God has asked you to do — in your marriage and family, in ministry or career and in all relationships.

When Belinda and I started to build a church, a group of denominational men came to me and said, "It will never happen. Everyone who has ever started to build a church like this in this city has failed. You can go ahead and give it a try if you want to, but it isn't going to happen."

That was like saying, "Go for it," to a blood hound! There is just something in me that enjoys a challenge, particularly if I know God is orchestrating the situation. It was faith on the rise in me building a picture. I wrote the vision down which God gave me before we ever started the church. Two months before we ever had our first service, I was saying, "I pastor Living Water Church, Tampa, Florida."

The first Sunday we had 75 people, and they threw me out of the denomination the next week, saying, "You're out of here. It's not supposed to work. We don't want you preaching that faith stuff." Praise God! I can do all things through Christ.

Six years later, we have a congregation of some 1,500 people. The same denomination that wouldn't support me, invited me back, but now I have another association as my spiritual authority and covering. The Association of Faith Churches and Ministers (A.F.C.M.) led by my good friend, Dr. Jim Kaseman and his lovely wife Kathi. I said to the denominational leader, "There are other brethren who need you, but we are still in the same family." I love the people in that denominational group and they are doing a great work for God, but I have joined hands with those of like precious faith (2 Pet. 1:1). **Can two walk together, unless they are agreed?** (Amos 3:3)

What is it that the devil has told you that you can't do? What has he said will never happen? That's the very thing God wants you to go for. Whatever the devil is telling you that you can't do or can't have, as long as it is legitimate and righteous, go for it!

Maybe you've heard Satan say, "You will never get out of debt." It is true that I would never get out of debt if I wasn't a child of God, but I am a child of God. I can do all things with God's help (Phil. 4:13). "Yes, but you're in a mess and you created it." Yes, and by God's grace and mercy, He will give me the ability to get out of debt.

I used to mock people who played golf, and then I had someone tell me I wouldn't be able to play the game very well. That bugged me, so I started to play. I couldn't do it very well, but I have been working at it! I just keep going. I get so frustrated with that old golf club at times that an imagination builds in me: "The next hole, you will hit it 700 times and it still won't go in." When that imagination comes, I say, "Absolutely not. I can do anything I want to do as long as God is in it." I am going to play golf, and I am going to be good at it, because whatever is worthy of my time, I am going to do it right. I am not there yet, but I will be!

If you are going to do something, don't just do it. Do everything as unto the Lord as Paul said in Colossians 3:23. **And whatever you do, do it heartily, as to the Lord and not to men.** Let's do it all well. Do it for Jesus and be good at it!

Mark 11:23 says, **Whoever...believes that those things he says will be done, he will have whatever he says.** Speaking your mind with no Holy Spirit control over your tongue will take you straight to the bottom! An unrenewed mind is a ticket to failure. Speak God's mind. His Word and

His mind are one and the same. With a renewed mind you will be able to put on the new man and the old man will stay buried.

Begin to confess what God says about you. "I have the mind of Christ. I am a new man with new thoughts, new ways of dealing with problems. I am more than a conqueror. Nothing can stop me. I can do all things through Christ Who strengthens me. I am an overcomer. I am the head and not the tail. I am going over, not under. God's blessings are overtaking me to the point I am able to lend and not borrow. I am blessed coming in and going out. The Lord causes my enemies who come against me to be defeated before my face. They come against me one way and flee before me seven ways. All of the work of my hands is blessed." (Deut. 28:1-13.)

9
Cleaning Up Stinking Thinking!

The words you speak today will frame your tomorrow with good or with bad, just as God framed the worlds with His words (Heb. 11:3).

Satan whips many people by defeating them in their thoughts about the past. How can he stick your nose in something that doesn't exist anymore? It only exists in your mind. When there is genuine repentance, the pages of your past are torn out of God's book. Repentance gives you the opportunity to unhook the caboose and leave it behind!

You can change present thought patterns by following Bible principles. There are some things you can never change, like the leopard cannot change his spots. If you are black, you can't change your skin color. You will be black until you go to heaven. If you are white, you are going to be white all the way to the end. If you were born in a certain hospital, you will never change that. You will never change your natural parents.

Death is a situation that once the person is in eternity cannot be changed. It creates crisis. My mother died when I was in second grade, so it particularly created a crisis for my dad. Anyone facing the crisis of death should realize, "This is a time where God will carry you. You can't change the situation."

I asked my dad, "Did God carry you?" He said, "Absolutely. People need to hear that they are going to make it and that God has the ability to sustain them."

Change what you can change and forget what you can't change. Whatever you can't change has no power to stop you, because if it could, God would give you the ability to change it.

If there is something that stands between you and the goal God has given you, He will give you the ability to change it. If you can't change it, then it's not something that can stop you and you should not spend time worrying about it. If you were born in the ghetto, get the ghetto out of you. The problem is that people get a ghetto mentality, a poverty mentality, or a shortage mentality in them. Poverty isn't bound by skin color, so you can unhook from poverty, whether you are white, black, yellow, or any other color. Skin color isn't the issue. It's what is in you that counts.

You can change learned behaviors and habits. We're going to forget the leopard spots for now and deal with learned behavior. Personality is the habitual patterns and qualities of behavior as expressed by mental and physical activities and attitudes.

Proverbs 22:6 says, **Train up a child in the way he should go, and when he is old he will not depart from it.**

I am teaching Amanda, my little daughter, to pray every time there are symptoms of sickness so prayer will become an established pattern with her. Where I used to reach for the medicine cabinet, the first thing she will do is reach out her hand in healing. Why? It will become a part of her personality. That habit will be ingrained in her. She will think healing when symptoms come.

Your character is the reputation of your personality and the patterns you have developed. To say, "He is a man of character," means he has a reputation of a good pattern of behavior. If you see a person who once was a thief and now is a man of upstanding business, all that has changed is a pattern and it began with his thoughts.

Cleaning Up Stinking Thinking!

When I was born again, my dad said to me, "Prove to me that you are really a different person." You couldn't have hit me harder with a baseball bat up the side of my head. I was so disappointed, but the Holy Spirit whispered to me, "You will." What was my dad looking for? A character change. He was looking for a new reputation for me.

People are looking for a real character change, not just a change in our personality. Sometimes you can express your personality in different ways, but your character and your reputation are hard to change, because they require a complete change of patterns of thinking and of behavior.

Today, some sixteen years later, my family acknowledges that I am a new man. The evidence of my spiritual experience is a change in my heart and my character! Old things have passed away, and all things have become new.

Before you change, you must believe you can change. As long as you don't believe you can change, nothing will happen. The greatest challenge I have in any kind of counseling, preaching, or ministering to people is convincing them that they can change. If you don't believe you can change, then there is nothing I can do for you. The laying on of hands won't change you unless you believe it will change you. You must believe that God is bigger than your bad habits and wrong thoughts and that He can change them.

In Ephesians 4, Paul is dealing with change.

> **This I say, therefore, and testify in the Lord, that you should no longer walk as the rest of the Gentiles walk, in the futility of their mind,**
>
> **Having their understanding darkened, being alienated from the life of God.**
>
> **Ephesians 4:17,18**

A born-again believer cannot be alienated from the life of God, because His life is in you. **Because of the ignorance that is in them** (Verse 18). You aren't ignorant. You need to say to yourself, "I have the mind of Christ."

Verse 17 says, **No longer walk as the rest of the Gentiles walk, in the futility of their mind.** Bad habits controlled the Gentiles. They became who they were through practice. If, as a Christian, you say you can't change, then you deny the reality of Who resides within you. Paul was saying, "Do not walk after the pattern of the Gentiles."

If you believe you cannot change bad habits, then God is powerless in your life. If it is impossible for a Christian to live right and to fulfill every righteous requirement, not only of the law but of faith, then what you are believing is powerless.

First John 4:4 says, **He** [Jesus Christ] **who is in you is greater than he** [the devil] **who is in the world.** In the past, I could preach a hang-you-over-hell and singe-your-little-toe sermon and get you guilty enough to cause you to go to the altar and repent again. But the problem with me and a lot of others is that we would go to the altar and repent but leave the altar the same person. Repentance for us was appeasing God's wrath, not changing who we were.

I got saved hundreds of times. I was convinced that I had to earn God's love by the way I thought and the way I acted; but then faith in His grace changed my life. Habits that had hung on me like fishhooks fell off when I began to say, "They have no power over me; He who is in me is greater than he who is in the world."

I have changed drastically over the last few years as the revelation of faith has grown in my life. I now acknowledge that the Greater One lives in me and the old life doesn't have to be today's life. I think differently now.

If indeed you have heard Him and have been taught by Him, as the truth is in Jesus:

> **That you put off, concerning your former conduct, the old man which grows corrupt according to the deceitful lusts.**
>
> **Ephesians 4:21,22**

Satan is quick to say, "Look at the thoughts that have come to your mind. Why even try? Why fight it? You are never going to change. You will always be this way." That's the deceitfulness of lust. As long as you come into agreement with that thought and begin to speak it, you will never change. You set in motion a pattern of thinking that results in a reputation of your character.

When I was growing up, I was called Mr. Lazyboy, because I found every excuse I could not to do any work. That was my character. I went into the army, and I looked for ways to be lazy. It was a pattern. Now my problem is, I have to force myself to slow down. After I was born again, I broke that lazy pattern. I went too far the other way and worked a hundred hours a week. But now my strength is maintaining a healthy balance. If Satan couldn't fry me as a lazy bum, he was going to fry me as a *workaholic*.

The first four and a half years of our marriage, I couldn't go on vacation, because I was too important and too busy. I was glad not to be known as a lazy bum anymore. I was going to be known as somebody. The Kingdom couldn't go on without me! But I am feeling less guilty about going on vacation now than ever in my life. I am training myself in a new way of thinking.

Jesus Himself went off alone with His disciples to pray and rest, and He told me to do the same thing. We've got to break old patterns of thinking.

Some of our patterns of thinking will kill us if we don't change them. For years I was paranoid about going out in the sun. I am walking on the beach now. I lay hands on my face and skin and say, "Father, I thank You for protecting me from skin cancer in the name of Jesus."

I had a mole that started to look funny, and at first, fear ran through my brain telling me it was cancer. Belinda laid her hand on that thing and cursed it. It shriveled up to nothing. Even if I get it, I will be cured of it.

Some people fear exposure to AIDS by eating restaurant foods. You have a choice to do your own cooking and eat at home or develop your faith. The Bible says your food is sanctified by the Word and prayer (I Timothy 4:5).

Years ago a minister came to me and said, "I am quitting the ministry." I asked, "Why?" He said, "Because I can't stop lusting." I asked, "Do you have HBO in your home?" He said, "Yes." "Do you buy girly magazines?" "Sometimes." I said, "Give me six weeks. If we don't change this pattern in six weeks, then you can quit."

It took me two weeks to convince him that he could change. It only takes one day to break the habit. It started with removing the weakness from his house (Acts 19:18,19; 2 Cor. 6:17), but it takes twenty-one days to become comfortable with a new pattern of behavior. He had to begin to think victory. He is still in the ministry today.

When you get up in the morning, do you go through a certain ritual? You probably put your shoes, your trousers or dress and your make-up on the same way. You brush your teeth, one side first and then the other, then up and down and swish it around and gurgle and spit! Patterns! Patterns! Patterns! The stress that would be on you and me if we had to think through all of these things would break us. So God gives us the ability to do things over and over again without thinking about them.

I was so ingrained with feelings of unworthiness and inadequacy that when the board in our church (A.F.C.M.) who sets my salary gave me a raise, I'd give it away; not because I was being generous (I wish that had been my motive), but I was taught all my life that preachers weren't supposed to have any money. If they did, they were preaching for the wrong reason. That's stinking thinking!

Whole denominations have taken vows of poverty. How in the world are we going to reach the world if we are in poverty? The most effective thing the devil ever did to stop the church was to convince us that we shouldn't have anything, which is a pattern of stinking thinking!

I remember the first time a love offering was taken for us when we first started the church. It was at Christmas time. We received several hundred dollars. I felt so guilty. Six months later, I received a raise and gave it to the staff.

I was in a hotel in Montgomery, Alabama, with Dr. Jim Kaseman. After learning what I had done, He laid his hands on my head and said, "I pray Jesus, you heal Pastor Ron of a poverty mentality!" I stopped him and asked, "Why are you doing this to me?" He said, "Because your church will never rise above your vision of yourself. How can you lead people where you have never been?"

I'll be honest with you. I don't desire to be rich. I'm not seeking riches, but they are seeking me! The Bible says, **Those who desire to be rich fall into temptation and a snare** (1 Timothy 6:9). I used to think, "If preachers had money, they would end up tempted and snared."

There are ministers who have wrong motives and money is one of them. Some ministers are selling bottles of Jordan water for $15. If you buy it, you're an idiot! That water is no different than the bodies of water near you.

Have you heard this one? "Bless the Lord, I took a handkerchief to Jerusalem and rubbed it over the tomb where Jesus laid. If you will send $100, I will send you a piece of my hanky!" Forget it! That person is a charlatan!

God will go to great lengths to bring His riches to you when your motives, attitudes and thinking are right. At times I have been tempted to just pack it in, but I change my mind and it is changing my finances.

If you have declared bankruptcy, I am not putting any condemnation on you, but don't go bankrupt again. You don't have to go bankrupt. Bankruptcy means your heavenly account is empty. When you give, it is given back to you. God draws on what you have given. Interest is accumulated in heaven.

Jesus said:

> **Do not lay up for yourselves treasures on earth, where moth and rust destroy and where thieves break in and steal;**
>
> **But lay up for yourselves treasures in heaven, where neither moth nor rust destroys and where thieves do not break in and steal.**
>
> **For where your treasure is, there your heart will be also.**
>
> **Matthew 6:19-21**

God keeps the books. He issues the orders and the checks on your behalf, which means that when you have a need, you have a right to draw on what you have given. He pays a hundred-fold dividend.

If you are a giving person, you will never be able to use all that is accumulated on your behalf. One day you will walk across and see a big pile of money. You will ask, "What is that?" Jesus will say, "That's the interest off of what you have given. I have been trying to channel it to you, but you wouldn't take it."

You may think you are unworthy, but you are worthy simply because you are one of God's kids.

There are a lot of rich people who inherited from their father what they never worked to get and never deserved to get. They got it because of their name. God has great things for you because of the name He has given you.

Wilson and Amanda are my children, so they are entitled to everything I have.

In Luke 12:32, Jesus said, **It is your Father's good pleasure to give you the kingdom.** Nothing would please the Father more than for you to be so blessed that you would have enough to help other people. If your own needs aren't met, then God will never be able to use you to meet someone else's needs.

You need to change your way of thinking. Avoid such confessions as, "I am on a fixed income." Let God fix it. Keep believing. Don't limit God with the words of your own mouth. I received a check for $10,000 from an aunt I didn't even know I had.

A beetle lies on his back, helplessly kicking his feet in the air. What sort of change does he need? Some say he needs to be turned over. Everything seems to be okay until he falls over again. He tried to go down the same hill the same way and fell on his back again. What he really needs is to change the direction of his life.

When you do something long enough, it becomes a part of you. The first time you drove a car, you had to think about everything. After driving for a few years, when brake lights go on ahead of you, you don't think, "What should I do? Where's the manual?" You hit the brakes without even thinking.

The same process is involved in learning to walk by faith. The Word must become such a part of us that it flows out of us automatically, just as it did with Jesus when He said, "It is written." If something happens at work, you don't have time to go home and get the coffee table Bible and start searching through it. Hide the Word in your heart and speak it out of your own mouth. That's the best preparation for handling any crisis, for Isaiah 33:6 says, **Wisdom and knowledge [of God] will be the stability of your times.**

People get frustrated because they've got all these bad habits in their brain. They have been putting themselves down, calling themselves a failure. When you start infusing them with faith, it's like, "Put your hands on the wheel and turn the key on." But after a while, as they meditate upon the Word daily, applying it to their thoughts and circumstances, it changes their entire lives.

Afterword
By Dr. Roy H. Hicks

One will inevitably witness and experience many crises as a result of living in the world, as we have, for more than seventy years.

We have walked through tragedies and times of crisis with others, ministering all of the comfort we could as ministers. But in all of those years of ministry, we had not been confronted with the devastating, shocking telephone call that one of our children was suddenly killed.

On February 10, 1994, we were roused from sleep by a telephone call and told that our first-born son was killed in a plane crash. We had no premonition or any warning to be prepared for such a sudden, shocking phone call. The mind recoils. Right then, in that initial moment, you cannot grasp the reality of the fact that your loved one is dead...that you will not see him again in this life.

Your faith is where you are to place your focus. At times after such a situation, you will experience very deep emotions. They are very real and cannot be discounted, but do not let your emotions rule over you. Because we have replaced the emotions that tried to overcome us with praises to God, we can now deal with the many "aftershocks" that pictures, letters, tapes, etc. bring to mind.

Here are some of the things we have learned in our crisis which may be of help to you in your time of trial. Deal with the event from faith operating out of your heart, not with emotions. Speak the Word with thanksgiving, confessing what you believe, and guard against the "what ifs." Remember that praise will help you dominate every emotion and lead you into victory.

About the Author
By Dr. Roy H. Hicks

I have known Dr. Ron Clark for over five years. In those five years, I have observed not only his personal growth in the Lord and his ability to share the Word of God, but also the phenomenal growth of the Living Water Church.

I strongly recommend his words of counsel in this book about the times of crisis we experience.